SMART LADIES OF THE 21ST CENTURY

Eddie A. Opitz

Smart Ladies of the 21st Century:

Women Redefining Success and Shaping Industries

TABLE OF CONTENT

TABLE OF CONTENT 3
INTRODUCTION 7
Chapter 1 10
    Breaking the Glass Ceiling 10

    The Background of Women's Fight for Equality in History 13

    Women's Prejudices and Difficulties in A Variety of Fields 19

    Success Stories of Women Breaking Through and Reaching Leadership Positions 22

    Ways to get past challenges and progress professionally 25

Chapter 2 33
    Leading in Business and Entrepreneurship 33

    Accounts of Powerful Women in Leadership and Business 35

    Success Tales of Startups and Businesses Run by Women 39

    Creative Tactics Used by Women to Navigate the Corporate World 43

    Obstacles and Opportunities Facing Female Entrepreneurs 47

Networks and Resources for Prospective Female Business Owners 51

Chapter 3 .... **56**
Innovators in Science and Technology 56

Contributions of Women to STEM Fields 59

Innovation and Groundbreaking Findings Produced by Female Technologists and Scientists 65

Obstacles that Women in STEM Encounter and Tactics to Advance Gender Diversity 68

Women's Accomplishments STEM 72

Projects and Activities that Encourage Females to Pursue Careers in STEM 76

Chapter 4 .... **81**
Voices in Politics and Advocacy 81

Participation of Women in Government and Politics 84

Influence of Female Activists and Leaders on Human Rights and Social Justice 88

Success Stories of Women Using Advocacy and Political Engagement to Drive Change 95

Strategies for Increasing Women's Participation and Leadership in Public Life 99

Chapter 5 .... **105**

Cultural Icons and Creative Visionaries 105

Influence of Women in the Arts, Entertainment, and Media Industries 105

Trailblazing Actresses, Musicians, Writers, and Visual Artists 110

Impact of Female Cultural Icons on Shaping Perceptions and Challenging Stereotypes 114

Opportunities and Challenges Facing Women in the Creative Industries 117

Role of Women in Promoting Diversity and Inclusion in Cultural Settings. 121

Chapter 6 126
Navigating Work-Life Balance 126

Challenges Faced by Women in Balancing a Career, Family, and Personal Life 126

Strategies for Achieving Work-Life Balance and Prioritizing Self-care 130

The Significance of Policies and Workplaces that Empower Women 134

Success Stories of Women Who Have Found Work-life Balance and Fulfilment 138

Resources and Tips for Managing Work-Life Integration 142

Chapter 7 ....**148**
    Empowering Future Generations 148

    Importance of Mentorship, Education, and Community Support 152

    Project and Activities Empowering Young Girls and Women 156

    Mentors and Role Models Inspiring the Next Generation 160

    Strategies for Promoting Gender Equality and Empowering Girls 163

    Opportunities for Individuals and Organizations to Support Future Generations..167

Conclusion **171**
    References and Resources 173

    About the Author 175

INTRODUCTION

Women's roles have changed dramatically over history, moving from oppression to empowerment and from silence to resilience. Women have historically been marginalized, their voices silenced, and their aspirations thwarted by institutional and cultural constraints. But the 21st century has ushered in a new era of opportunity, one in which women have become dynamic change agents who are reshaping sectors, defying expectations, and making a lasting impression on the global scene.

As we work through the challenges of the contemporary era, it is clear that women are no longer willing to accept submissive roles or scarce chances. Equipped with intelligence, inventiveness, and an unyielding determination to make their mark in a world traditionally dominated by men, they have emerged as leaders in various industries. Women are becoming more visible in a variety of settings, including boardrooms, labs, political arenas, and artistic fields. They are doing so not just as symbols of diversity but also as vital contributors to advancement and success.

This book, **"Smart Ladies of the 21st Century,"** is a celebration of the remarkable accomplishments made by women worldwide. It is a celebration of their ability to bounce back from setbacks, inventiveness in aiming for greatness, and unwavering will to go above and beyond what is expected of them. We go on a journey through the pages of this book to discover the many roles and incredible contributions played by women in reshaping history and the very definition of success.

A distinct facet of women's empowerment and accomplishment is the focus of each chapter in this book. Women are at the forefront of change, pushing development and inspiring future generations. They are tearing down barriers like the glass ceiling in corporate hallways, spearheading scientific advancements, fighting for social justice, and changing cultural landscapes.

We are reminded of the strength of tenacity, the influence of creativity, and the value of unity in the pursuit of equality and justice as we read through the biographies of these astute women of the twenty-first century. Their experiences light the way for upcoming generations of women to follow, acting as inspirational and uplifting beacons.

We cordially invite you to embark with us on a voyage of exploration, illumination, and joy in the pages that follow. As we work to create a more welcoming, just, and powerful society for everybody, let's celebrate the accomplishments of women both past and present, and keep advocating for their rights.

With each turn of the page, may we be inspired to emulate the courage, tenacity, and brilliance of the smart ladies of the 21st century, and may their stories ignite a spark of hope and possibility in the hearts of all who dare to dream and aspire to greatness.

Chapter 1

Breaking the Glass Ceiling

The idea of the "glass ceiling" is a potent metaphor for the enduring obstacles that have impeded women's advancement in the workforce. Regardless of their skills or abilities, it is an imperceptible but powerful barrier that keeps women from rising to the top leadership positions. This symbolic wall has historically hampered women's career success, sustaining gender inequity and casting a shadow over their progress.

We set out to investigate the historical foundations of the women's labor movement for workplace equality in this chapter. Women have battled systematic inequities and societal standards that have limited them to subservient roles for a very long time, starting with the suffragette movement and continuing with the current fight for equal pay and representation. We explore the lives of well-known individuals who broke through glass ceilings and defied expectations, opening doors for the next generation of women to follow their dreams unhindered.

Furthermore, we face the unforgiving truths of the obstacles and prejudices that still affect women in a variety of fields. Within corporate boardrooms and scientific laboratories, women face a range of obstacles that hinder their career progression, from covert gender bias to more overt forms of discrimination. Women have overcome these challenges by using their abilities, fortitude, and willpower to forge successful careers in fields where males predominate.

We recognize the successes of women who have defied expectations and attained leadership positions in their respective areas throughout this exploration. Their experiences are inspirational tales that show how capable women may be in positions that have historically been filled by men. These trailblazing women, who range from trailblazing scientists to pioneering CEOs, have flipped stereotypes and changed the perception of what it means to be a leader in the twenty-first century.

Finally, our attention is directed toward strategies and information that enable women to surmount challenges and establish prosperous careers. Through the use of networking, mentoring, and organizational reform advocacy, women may question the status quo and promote more inclusive workplaces where fairness is the norm. Our mission is to empower women by providing them with inspirational tales and useful guidance, enabling them to face the professional world with resilience and self-assurance.

This chapter honors the resilience, bravery, and unyielding spirit of women who broke the glass ceiling. It serves as a reminder of their lasting influence as well as an appeal to the next generation to carry on the struggle for female empowerment and gender equality in all areas of society. With our combined efforts, we can break down the glass ceiling, remove obstacles, and create a future where women are free to lead and prosper.

Chapter Three expands the scope of our discussion to include influential women in science and technology. The innovative contributions made by female scientists and technologists, who are changing our perception of the world and progressing in their areas, will be discussed in this chapter. The STEM areas provide distinct obstacles for these women; nonetheless, their perseverance and ingenuity propel advancement and motivate transformation. We will expose the structural obstacles they face and draw attention to the impressive progress being made in the direction of a more inventive and inclusive future by looking at their groundbreaking endeavors. Come explore the narratives of these remarkable women, whose accomplishments are setting the path for the next wave of female scientists and technologists.

The Background of Women's Fight for Equality in History

There have been innumerable acts of bravery, resiliency, and tenacity over the centuries-long path towards gender equality. Women have long been leaders in the struggle for equal pay and representation in the workplace and in society at large, beginning with the suffragette movement in the late 19th and early 20th centuries.

In the fight for women's rights, the suffragette movement, which grew in strength in the late 19th century, was a turning point. Globally, women activists, such as Susan B. Anthony and Emmeline Pankhurst, dedicated their lives to securing the right to vote. Their courageous deeds, which included hunger strikes and nonviolent protests, upended the deeply ingrained patriarchal conventions of the day and cleared the path for women's suffrage in numerous nations.

Even with the suffragettes' historic victories, the fight for female equality was far from over. Women experienced bias and discrimination in the workplace during the 20th century, frequently being forced into lower-paying and less prominent roles than their male counterparts. Although the United States Equal Pay Act of 1963 marked a major advancement in resolving gender-based wage inequities, the same disadvantages still exist today.

The feminist movement, which emerged in the second part of the 20th century, served as a further impetus for efforts to remove structural obstacles that prevented women from advancing in society. Women's rights to work, education, and reproductive autonomy were among the causes those feminist researchers and activists fought for, as well as gender equality in a variety of social contexts. They also questioned conventional gender norms. Their unceasing campaigning changed the way that people talked about gender and set the stage for progressive legislative changes that supported the empowerment of women.

The fact that differences in representation and opportunity still exist despite these advancements highlights the ongoing difficulties that women in the workforce face. Women still face obstacles to their career advancement, such as unconscious prejudice, harassment at work, and the widespread belief that there is a "glass ceiling." To truly achieve gender parity in the workplace, there is still more work to be done, despite the efforts of corporations and legal measures to address these concerns.

Nonetheless, the background of women's fight for equality shows how resilient and tenacious women have been throughout history. Their combined efforts have cleared the path for advancement and motivated upcoming generations to carry on the battle for gender parity. We are reminded of the value of cooperation, advocacy, and group efforts as we consider the accomplishments to date and the obstacles still to be overcome in the creation of a more just and inclusive society.

Legendary Individuals Who Broke Down Boundaries and Cleared the Path for Upcoming Generations

Courageous women have accomplished amazing things throughout history by overcoming social expectations and the odds, setting an example for future generations. Distinguished individuals whose ground-breaking accomplishments broke through barriers and broadened the world of opportunities for women are included in this group of trailblazers.

The legendary scientist and chemist Marie Curie is revered in the annals of scientific history. She was not only the first woman to receive the Nobel Prize, but she is still the only individual to have done so in two distinct scientific domains: chemistry and physics. Curie's pioneering studies on radioactivity transformed contemporary physics and served as the basis for several other scientific breakthroughs. Her unrelenting dedication to her trade and relentless pursuit of information challenged preconceived preconceptions about women's intellectual capacities, paving the way for future generations of female scientists.

Fearless aviator and adventurer Amelia Earhart captivated the world's attention with her audacious aerial feats. Her achievement of being the first woman to fly solo across the Atlantic Ocean in 1932 cemented her place in aviation history as a trailblazer. Numerous women have been motivated to seek professions in aviation and other fields by Amelia Earhart's fearless attitude and will to push the envelope of what was thought to be achievable. Her legacy lives on as a tribute to the strength of tenacity and the limitless ability of women to surpass expectations and achieve greatness.

These well-known individuals are but a small sample of the innumerable women who have broken down barriers and made history in industries where men predominate. Women around the world continue to question the status quo and advance development in their various sectors, from Malala Yousafzai, the youngest Nobel Prize laureate, who relentlessly works for girls' education, to Rosa Parks, whose fearless act of defiance ignited the civil rights movement.

Their experiences serve as potent reminders of the transformational power that women possess when given the chance to flourish. These trailblazing women have cleared the path for future generations to follow their passions and reach their full potential, free from limitations, by dismantling barriers and dispelling prejudices.

We are motivated to continue these legendary people's courageous, tenacious, and resilient legacy as we honor their accomplishments. Their experiences serve as a reminder that no challenge is insurmountable and that gender is irrelevant in the quest for success. By recognizing their efforts, we also pay tribute to the many women who persist in defying expectations, breaking down barriers, and redefining what it means to be a woman in the twenty-first century.

Women's Prejudices and Difficulties in A Variety of Fields

Women still face numerous institutional obstacles and biases in the workplace, which limit their possibilities for leadership and success and obstruct their growth despite the tremendous progress made toward gender equality. These obstacles continue to impede women's career advancement and sustain gender inequality in a variety of sectors and organizational contexts.

Unconscious bias is a common issue that women encounter, particularly in the recruiting, promotion, and performance review processes. According to research, people frequently hold unconscious biases and stereotypes based on gender, which causes them to make biased decisions that favor males over equally capable women. Subtle examples of this bias include favoring male candidates for leadership positions or attributing women's accomplishments to chance rather than skill.

In addition, women frequently have unequal access to resources and opportunities in comparison to men. This inequality is especially noticeable in fields where males have historically held the majority of positions. In these fields, women may not have access to career development programs, mentorship opportunities, or professional networks. The inability of women to grow in their jobs and compete on an equal basis with their male colleagues can be attributed to a lack of access to essential resources and support networks.

The issue of gender pay disparity persists since women get paid less than men for doing equivalent or similar labor. Even with laws like the Equal Pay Act and other anti-discrimination statutes designed to address pay gaps, women are still paid much less than men in a variety of sectors and professions. In addition to reflecting larger differences in financial stability and economic opportunity, this wage disparity feeds cycles of inequality that impact women all their lives.

Moreover, in both public and corporate contexts, women are frequently underrepresented in senior leadership positions. In addition to limiting women's access to decision-making authority, a lack of gender diversity in leadership posts feeds preconceived notions about women's competence and aptitude for such positions. These prejudices, which have their roots in antiquated ideas about gender roles and expectations, make it harder for women to succeed professionally and advance in their careers.

Apart from these systemic obstacles, misconceptions and prejudices regarding women's capacities and leadership potential also pose a challenge. Women are frequently thought to be less capable, ambitious, and able to take on leadership responsibilities than men, despite evidence to the contrary. The aforementioned prejudices pose further obstacles for women aspiring to progress in their professions, compelling them to surmount self-doubt and demonstrate their merit using remarkable achievements and perseverance.

In conclusion, prejudices and difficulties women encounter in the workplace are complex and profoundly embedded in social norms and corporate cultures. To address these problems, it will take a concentrated effort to remove structural obstacles, confront unconscious prejudices, and build more inclusive and fair work environments where everyone, regardless of gender, has the chance to prosper. We cannot create a more just and equitable society where women are genuinely empowered to realize their full potential unless we acknowledge and address these issues head-on.

Success Stories of Women Breaking Through and Reaching Leadership Positions

Women have continuously shown their tenacity, willpower, and extraordinary skills in shattering the glass ceiling and achieving leadership roles in a variety of professions, even in the face of significant obstacles. From scientific labs to political arenas, from corporate boardrooms to entrepreneurial endeavors, women have forged successful careers and dispelled preconceptions in the process. Their experiences are striking examples of the transforming power of female leadership and the unbounded ability of women to achieve success in their chosen industries.

One noteworthy success story is that of Indra Nooyi, the former CEO of PepsiCo, who rose to the top of the corporate ladder due to her innovative leadership. During her tenure, Nooyi, a visionary strategist and creative thinker, turned PepsiCo into a worldwide powerhouse by deftly navigating the complexity of the beverage and snack industries. She received international recognition and cemented her reputation as one of the most significant corporate executives of her time with her strategic vision, dedication to sustainability, and emphasis on diversity and inclusion. Nooyi's incredible journey from a young child in India to a Fortune 500 CEO inspires women everywhere by showing the value of tenacity, resiliency, and unflinching drive to accomplish one's objectives.

Angela Merkel, the German Chancellor and a trailblazer in the field of European politics, is another outstanding person. As the first female chancellor of Germany, Angela Merkel has commanded enormous clout on the international scene thanks to her steady hand, practical outlook, and steadfast dedication to democratic principles. Throughout her career, she has handled difficult geopolitical situations, financial crises, and societal changes with poise and determination, winning the respect and admiration of both citizens and foreign leaders. In addition to changing the course of German politics, Merkel's unwavering leadership and inclusive governance approach have encouraged women all over the world to pursue leadership and influence roles.

These are only a few of the countless women who have overcome obstacles and cracked glass ceilings in their respective areas. Women continue to push the envelope and redefine what is possible, as seen by Ursula Burns, the first African American woman to run a Fortune 500 firm, and Kamala Harris, the first female vice president of the United States. Their accomplishments serve as potent reminders of the transformative power of female leadership and the necessity of establishing more equal and inclusive work environments where women may flourish.

We pay tribute to the bravery, tenacity, and resolve of individuals who have blazed the path for later generations of women to follow by honoring the success stories of women making waves. Their experiences act as inspirational lights that point us in the direction of a day when gender equality is an actual thing rather than simply a pipe dream. Let us take courage from the experiences of these trailblazing women and fight relentlessly to create a world in which every woman has the chance to realize her full potential as we push for increased representation, inclusion, and women's empowerment.

Ways to get past challenges and progress professionally

Women may find it difficult to navigate the complex corporate landscape, but with the correct tools and networks in place, they can overcome challenges and steer clear of trouble. This section delves into various crucial tactics that women can utilize to surpass the glass ceiling and progress in their professions. Additionally, it covers measures that companies can take to establish more fair and inclusive work environments.

One crucial strategy for women is to build strong networks and cultivate meaningful relationships within their professional circles. By establishing connections with colleagues, mentors, and industry peers, women can gain valuable insights, access new opportunities, and expand their support systems. Networking events, professional organizations, and online platforms offer valuable avenues for women to connect with like-minded individuals and build mutually beneficial relationships that can help propel their careers forward.

Seeking sponsorship and guidance is another crucial strategy for women who want to break through barriers and succeed in their jobs. Mentors can help women overcome obstacles and take advantage of growth possibilities by offering direction, counsel, and support based on their own experiences. Conversely, sponsors actively support women's progress inside their companies by giving them access to senior positions, high-profile initiatives, and promotions. Through fostering connections with mentors and sponsors, women can obtain invaluable assistance and direction while navigating the intricacies of the business world.

Additionally, self-advocacy is essential for women who want to surpass the glass ceiling and succeed in their careers. Women must take the initiative to articulate their accomplishments, abilities, and goals and to champion opportunities that correspond with their professional goals. This could entail aggressively pursuing leadership positions within their organizations, speaking out during meetings, and looking for stretch assignments. Women may show their worth and set themselves up for success in the workplace by taking charge of their career pathways and speaking out for themselves.

Furthermore, by putting diversity and inclusion policies into action, addressing unconscious bias, and encouraging gender-balanced leadership, organizations play a critical role in fostering more equal workplaces for women. Initiatives that help reduce obstacles to women's advancement and foster a more welcoming and encouraging work environment for all employees include diversity training, programs that raise awareness of unconscious prejudice, and flexible work schedules. Organizations can also work towards gender parity in leadership roles by putting in place policies that support gender inclusion and diversity at all organizational levels.

In conclusion, eliminating the barriers that prevent women from advancing in the corporate sector calls for a multidimensional strategy that blends individual tactics with organizational measures. Through establishing robust networks, pursuing sponsorship and mentorship, standing up for oneself, and encouraging inclusivity and diversity in the workplace, women can surpass the glass ceiling and realize their complete potential. Let's collaborate to build a future where women have the tools they need to excel in all facets of their professional lives.

Examples:

1. Anecdote: In an interview, Facebook COO Sheryl Sandberg discussed her experiences navigating the obstacles faced by women in technology and provided advice on how to combat gender bias in the workplace.

2. Quote: "Success is not about climbing the corporate ladder; it's about creating your ladder and inviting others to climb with you." Oprah Winfrey is a media mogul and philanthropist.

3. Case Study: Company X implemented a diversity and inclusion initiative aimed at increasing the representation of women in leadership positions. By offering leadership development programs, mentorship opportunities, and flexible work arrangements, the company saw a significant increase in the number of women in senior leadership roles within two years.

4. Anecdote: German Chancellor Angela Merkel talked about how she overcame gender prejudice and mistrust from her male colleagues to become well-known in European politics. As a result of her tenacity and astute leadership, Merkel rose to prominence in the global political arena.

5. Quotation: "Diversity is not just a buzzword; it's a strategic imperative for business success in the 21st century." The former CEO of PepsiCo, Indra Nooyi.

6. Case Study: Company Y implemented a bias training program for hiring managers to address unconscious biases in recruitment and promotion processes. As a result, the company saw an increase in the diversity of its workforce and improved employee satisfaction and retention rates.

7. Anecdote: Serena Williams, a professional tennis player and businesswoman, talked about how she overcame discrimination and hardship in the predominantly male sports world to become one of the best athletes in history.

8. Quote from: "Leadership is not about gender; it's about vision, integrity, and the ability to inspire others." New Zealand Prime Minister Jacinda Ardern.

9. Case Study: Company Z implemented a parental leave policy that offered equal benefits to both mothers and fathers, promoting gender equality and work-life balance. The policy

resulted in higher employee morale, productivity, and retention rates.

10. Anecdote: Education campaigner and Nobel laureate Malala Yousafzai talked about her brave journey of fighting against the Taliban's ban on girls' education in Pakistan and promoting the rights of girls everywhere.

These examples highlight the range of perspectives and experiences held by successful female CEOs and companies committed to promoting equal opportunity in the workplace. Through tales, quotations, and case studies, they offer enlightening knowledge and inspiration for individuals and organizations seeking to promote more equitable and inclusive work environments.

This chapter provides a thorough analysis of the challenges and triumphs faced by women who have broken through the glass ceiling for readers who wish to thrive in their careers.

33 | SMART LADIES OF THE 21ST CENTURY

Chapter 2

Leading in Business and Entrepreneurship

Although men have traditionally dominated the commercial and entrepreneurial spheres, this is beginning to change as more and more women make their voices heard and demonstrate their abilities. This chapter takes us inside the world of powerful women entrepreneurs and leaders— people who have broken through glass ceilings and disregarded ingrained conventions to become trailblazers in their industries. As they negotiate the complex world of business, these women represent resilience, ingenuity, and unflinching determination in everything from startup incubators to corporate boardrooms.

In the past, prejudices and systematic obstacles have prevented women from pursuing leadership roles and business prospects. But things are changing; stereotypes are being questioned by more and more women, and they are making room for themselves in fields that have historically been controlled by men. Through their experiences, we can observe the transforming force of perseverance in the face of difficulty, the limitless imagination that inspires invention, and the unwavering will that drives people to overcome challenges and grasp chances.

We learn about the personal experiences of these powerful women leaders and business owners, as well as the larger cultural changes that have facilitated their ascent to fame. These women exemplify the spirit of entrepreneurship and encourage others to follow their passions with boldness and conviction. They range from trailblazing CEOs who have transformed industries to visionary startup founders who have reshaped marketplaces.

We learn about the various approaches, difficulties, and victories that characterize the female entrepreneur's journey through their combined experiences. These people show resiliency and resourcefulness in the face of hardship, from overcoming gender bias to managing funding hurdles. As a result, they open the door for future generations of women to follow their entrepreneurial goals with confidence and drive.

We honor these powerful women leaders and entrepreneurs' tenacious energy and unshakable dedication to blazing successful routes in the face of overwhelming hurdles by recognizing their accomplishments. Their experiences are inspirational tales that point us in the direction of a day when diversity and gender equality will rule the corporate and entrepreneurial landscape. Let's set off on an exploratory and educational adventure together as we reveal the unsung tales of tenacity, inventiveness, and resolve that characterize the world of women in business and entrepreneurship.

Accounts of Powerful Women in Leadership and Business

This section delves into the motivational tales of prominent female entrepreneurs and leaders who have transformed industries and broken-down barriers with their steadfast perseverance and visionary leadership.

General Motors CEO Mary Barra: Mary Barra's rise to the top of General Motors, one of the biggest automakers in the world, is evidence of her extraordinary strategic and leadership abilities. Being the first female CEO of a significant international carmaker, Barra has taken the lead in promoting diversity, sustainability, and innovation inside the organization. Under her direction, General Motors has embraced cutting-edge technology like autonomous and electric cars, setting the business up for future expansion and success in a sector that is changing quickly.

Oprah Winfrey, media mogul and philanthropist: Her rise from poverty to prominence in the media sector is a credit to her fortitude, perseverance, and steadfast dedication to uplifting others. Oprah Winfrey, the creator of Harpo Productions and the Oprah Winfrey Network (OWN), has changed the talk show genre and the media landscape with her genuineness, empathy, and capacity to connect with viewers. In addition to her vast media empire, Winfrey is an ardent philanthropist who uses her influence to promote social justice, women's empowerment, and education.

Former Senior Vice President of Apple Retail Angela Ahrendts: Angela Ahrendts's creative approach to retail strategy and customer experience has defined her term as Senior Vice President of Apple Retail. Under her direction, Apple's retail locations developed into hubs of innovation and community, providing immersive experiences and promoting interpersonal relationships, in addition to being locations to purchase goods. The retail industry has transformed, with new benchmarks for customer engagement and brand loyalty established by Ahrendts' focus on empathy, authenticity, and human-centric design.

Sara Blakely, the founder of Spanx: Her journey from door-to-door fax machine sales to becoming the youngest self-made female billionaire is a monument to her inventiveness and spirit of entrepreneurship. Blakely, the creator of Spanx, transformed the undergarment market with her cutting-edge shapewear lines, enabling ladies to feel and look their best. Blakely is an inspiration to young entrepreneurs everywhere because of her unwavering dedication to realizing her vision and her courage to take calculated chances and accept failure.

Gwynne Shotwell, SpaceX's president and COO: The success of SpaceX as a leader in the aerospace sector may be attributed in large part to Gwynne Shotwell's leadership. Shotwell is in charge of all facets of SpaceX's operations as president and chief operating officer, including the creation and launch of ground-breaking space technologies like the Dragon spacecraft and Falcon rockets. She has led SpaceX to unprecedented heights with her strategic vision, operational know-how, and innovation-driven dedication, opening up new avenues for human space exploration and motivating the next generation of scientists and engineers.

These biographies only scratch the surface of the remarkable accomplishments of powerful female entrepreneurs and leaders who have broken down barriers and paved the way for others in their fields. They have reshaped what is possible for women in business and entrepreneurship via their leadership, ingenuity, and tenacity, creating a long legacy of empowerment and inspiration for future generations.

Success Tales of Startups and Businesses Run by Women

This section tells the amazing stories of women-owned businesses and startups who, through pure drive, ingenuity, and visionary leadership, have changed markets, overcome adversity, and achieved remarkable success.

Spanx, founded by Sara Blakely

The story of Sara Blakely, who went from being a struggling businesswoman to the head of a billion-dollar shapewear company, embodies the American Dream. In 2000, Blakely founded Spanx with barely $5,000 in savings and a daring goal to transform the knickers market. Blakely persevered in the face of many rejections and obstacles, using her imagination, ingenuity, and unflinching will to successfully launch her line of cutting-edge shapewear items. Spanx is a well-known worldwide brand today for its creative designs that enable women of all shapes and sizes to feel and look their best.

Emily Weiss, the founder of Glossier, is a disruptive beauty brand valued at over $1 billion. Her journey from a beauty blogger to the company's founder is a tribute to the strength of community-driven innovation. Inspired by her experiences as a beauty editor and the comments from her devoted fans, Weiss founded Glossier in 2014 to produce approachable, inclusive skincare and makeup products that honor uniqueness and genuineness. Using astute social media promotion, collaboratively created products, and an unwavering emphasis on client interaction, Glossier has fostered a loyal following and accomplished swift expansion and prosperity inside the very competitive beauty sector.

Rent the Runway was founded by Jennifer Hyman and Jennifer Fleiss in 2009 as a means of democratizing fashion and upending the established retail model. Customers may access high-end fashion at a significantly reduced price by renting designer apparel and accessories from the creative fashion rental platform for special occasions. Hyman and Fleiss persisted in the face of logistical difficulties in growing the firm and investor skepticism, turning Rent the Runway into a billion-dollar enterprise that has revolutionized the way consumers view and use fashion.

Julie Wainwright founded The RealReal

The RealReal was founded in 2011 as a result of Julie Wainwright's ambition to establish a marketplace for certified premium consignment products. With an emphasis on sustainability and authenticity, the online portal provides a carefully chosen assortment of pre-owned luxury goods, including fine jewelry, watches, and designer clothes and accessories. RealReal has toppled the old retail paradigm and brought about significant change in the fashion industry by being the go-to destination for luxury resale. This has been made possible by innovative technology, skilled authentication methods, and a commitment to openness.

Bumble Founded by Whitney Wolfe Herd

In 2014, Bumble was established as a result of Whitney Wolfe Herd's goal to transform online dating and empower women. By empowering women to start conversations and questioning established gender norms, the female-led dating app promotes an inclusive and courteous online dating environment.

Since its debut, Bumble has added networking and friend-finding tools to its dating offering, advancing its goal of giving women a platform to confidently pursue their goals and meaningful connections.

These inspirational tales of female-led enterprises and entrepreneurship show how female innovation and entrepreneurship are revolutionizing a variety of sectors, including technology, retail, and the beauty and fashion industries. These women have not only achieved incredible success but have also encouraged upcoming generations of entrepreneurs to dream big, defy expectations, and leave their mark on the world via their vision, tenacity, and unwavering pursuit of perfection.

Creative Tactics Used by Women to Navigate the Corporate World

Women entrepreneurs show incredible tenacity and creativity in negotiating the complexities of the business environment, even in the face of particular hurdles. To overcome challenges and grab opportunities in a constantly changing market, women have used creative approaches to establish and grow their enterprises. These methods have allowed them to capitalize on their unique perspectives and talents.

Leveraging digital technologies

By harnessing digital technologies, female entrepreneurs are expanding their reach, optimizing workflows, and improving client experiences. Women-led companies are adopting digital innovation to connect with customers, increase sales, and stand out in crowded markets. Examples of these innovations include social media marketing and e-commerce platforms. Women entrepreneurs can level the playing field and successfully compete with bigger, more established rivals by utilizing digital tools and platforms.

Embracing Collaboration and Community Building

Women business owners understand the importance of community development and teamwork in promoting creativity and business expansion. To overcome obstacles and take advantage of possibilities, women-led firms are utilizing the combined knowledge, resources, and support of their peers, whether through collaborations with other companies, involvement in online communities, or networking events. Women entrepreneurs can increase their influence in the business environment, gain access to new markets, and share best practices by developing strong networks and collaborative ties.

Prioritizing Diversity and Inclusion

Recognizing the benefits of varied viewpoints and experiences in fostering creativity and success, female entrepreneurs are leading the charge in promoting diversity and inclusion as core values in their companies.

Women-led companies may better understand and meet the demands of a wide range of consumer groups, stimulate creativity and innovation, and draw in top talent by cultivating inclusive cultures and diverse teams. Women entrepreneurs may also distinguish their companies, develop a devoted clientele, and have a good social influence in their communities by putting diversity and inclusion before anything else.

Seeking alternative funding sources

Alternative funding methods, such as grants, crowdfunding, and impact investing, are being investigated by female entrepreneurs in addition to conventional venture capital and angel investment. In addition to giving them access to financing that might be more in line with their goals and ideals, these alternative funding methods give female entrepreneurs more freedom, flexibility, and control over their companies. Women entrepreneurs can overcome the obstacles of money limits and gender bias by pursuing a variety of funding sources, which can also open up new avenues for growth and expansion.

Embracing Sustainable and Purpose-Driven Business Models

Sustainable, purpose-driven company models that give equal weight to financial gains and social and environmental effects are becoming more and more popular among women entrepreneurs. Women entrepreneurs may attract socially conscious consumers, distinguish their brands, and generate long-term value for stakeholders by connecting their businesses with ideals such as sustainability, social responsibility, and ethical practices. Women entrepreneurs can also spur innovation, cut expenses, and lower risks in a world market that is becoming more unstable and uncertain by incorporating sustainability into their business plans.

Women entrepreneurs are utilizing creative approaches to successfully negotiate the challenges of the corporate world and bring about significant transformations within their sectors. Women entrepreneurs are redefining success and reshaping the business landscape to be more inclusive, equitable, and sustainable through utilizing digital technologies, valuing networking and collaboration, putting diversity and inclusion first, looking for alternate sources of funding, and adopting sustainable and purpose-driven business models.

Obstacles and Opportunities Facing Female Entrepreneurs

Women entrepreneurs continue to encounter a variety of chances that can help them succeed in their ventures, in addition to enduring hurdles that have hindered them in the past, despite recent tremendous progress. This section explores the opportunities and obstacles that influence the status of women in entrepreneurship.

Challenges Facing Women in Entrepreneurship

1. Access to Capital: Finding the money needed to finance their businesses is one of the biggest obstacles facing female entrepreneurs. In the investment community, women frequently receive less money than men due to

a combination of gender bias among investors and a lack of networks and contacts. The unequal distribution of capital hinders women-led firms' capacity to develop, scale, and effectively compete in the market.

2. Gender Bias and Stereotypes: Women who run their businesses often face prejudice and stereotypes based on their gender, which damages their reputations and leadership skills. Women have enormous obstacles to obtaining respect and recognition in male-dominated fields, ranging from covert prejudice at investor meetings to overt discrimination in commercial transactions. In addition to questioning society's norms and expectations, overcoming these prejudices necessitates promoting greater equality and representation in entrepreneurial ecosystems.

3. Work-Life Balance: Women entrepreneurs may find it especially difficult to juggle the

demands of their businesses with their personal and family obligations. Burnout and stress can result from the pressures of operating a business, in addition to social expectations around childcare and housework. Setting limits, prioritizing self-care, and utilizing support systems to effectively handle conflicting demands are all necessary to achieve work-life balance.

Opportunities for Women in Entrepreneurship:

1. Access to Networks and Mentorship: To assist their professional development, women entrepreneurs can take advantage of a multitude of networks and mentorship programs. These networks provide helpful tools, direction, and contacts that can assist women in navigating the entrepreneurial journey and overcoming obstacles. They range from industry organizations to peer support groups and mentorship platforms.

2. Support Programs and Resources: Women entrepreneurs have access to a wide range of resources and support programs, such as entrepreneurship training programs, accelerators, and incubators. With the support of these programs, women can establish profitable companies and prosper in competitive industries by having access to capital, networking opportunities, mentorship, and skill development.

3. Rising Demand for Women-Led Enterprises: As the advantages of assisting women-led enterprises become more widely acknowledged, there is a rise in the market for the goods and services these women entrepreneurs provide. Diversity, accessibility, and gender equality are becoming more and more important to consumers, investors, and legislators. This opens up new chances for women to

demonstrate their abilities, spur innovation, and gain market share.

Women entrepreneurs still confront many obstacles on their path to success, but they also have access to a variety of resources and networks of support that can assist them in overcoming these obstacles. Through tackling concerns like financial accessibility, gender inequality, and juggling work and personal obligations, as well as capitalizing on networking opportunities, mentorship, and the growing market for women-owned enterprises, female entrepreneurs can reach their maximum potential and make valuable contributions to an entrepreneurial ecosystem that is more equitable, inclusive, and prosperous.

Networks and Resources for Prospective Female Business Owners

To help ambitious female entrepreneurs get the information, skills, and networks they need to succeed in their ventures, we have provided a thorough summary of the many resources and support systems that are out there in the following part.

1. Accelerators and Incubators:

Early-stage entrepreneurs can get resources, finance, and mentorship from programs like Y Combinator, Techstars, and 500 Startups to help them grow and expand.

Women-focused incubators and accelerators, such as Women's Startup Lab, the Female Founders Alliance, and Springboard Enterprises, provide resources and specialized support to female-led businesses, addressing the particular challenges faced by female entrepreneurs.

2. Networking Groups and Communities:

Networking events, workshops, and peer support groups are provided by organizations such as Women Entrepreneurs Inc. (WE-Incubate), Women Who Startup, and Elevate Network to enable women entrepreneurs to interact, cooperate, and exchange resources.

Virtual platforms are accessible via online networks and forums, like Women in Business Community (WIBC),

SheWorx, and Women 2.0, to enable female entrepreneurs to share ideas, get guidance, and obtain important resources and chances.

3. Mentorship Programs:

Through mentoring programs like the Women's Business Development

Centre (WBDC), SCORE Mentors, and the Cherie Blair Foundation for Women, aspiring female entrepreneurs are paired with seasoned mentors who offer support, direction, and advice throughout their entrepreneurial journey.

Women in Tech Mentoring, Women in STEM Mentoring, and Women in Finance Mentoring are examples of industry-specific mentorship programs that provide specialized assistance and direction to female entrepreneurs in specific fields.

4. Educational Resources and Training Programs:

Women entrepreneurs may learn vital business skills like marketing, finance, and leadership at an accessible and inexpensive price by participating in online courses, workshops, and educational resources like Coursera, Udemy, and LinkedIn Learning.

Business development initiatives that support women entrepreneurs in expanding and growing their companies include Goldman Sachs 10,000 Small Businesses, EY Entrepreneurial Winning Women, and Dell Women's Entrepreneur Network (DWEN). These initiatives offer comprehensive training, networking opportunities, and mentorship.

5. Funding Opportunities:

Women-focused venture capital firms invest in female-led startups and offer access to funding, mentorship, and strategic support. Examples of these firms are the Female Founders Fund, BBG Ventures, and Aspect Ventures.

Non-dilutive money is provided to women entrepreneurs through grant programs like the Eileen Fisher Women-

Owned Business Grant Program, Cartier Women's Initiative Awards, and Amber Grant for Women, which promote their businesses' innovation and growth.

With so many resources and support systems at their disposal, aspiring female entrepreneurs can achieve their goals of becoming successful business owners. Women entrepreneurs can acquire the information, abilities, and networks required to thrive in the cutthroat world of entrepreneurship by utilizing incubators and accelerators, networking groups and communities, mentorship programs, educational resources, and financial options. A more welcoming, varied, and dynamic entrepreneurial ecosystem—one in which women may prosper and leave a lasting impression on the world—is made possible by the combined efforts of these resources and support systems.

Women are becoming more and more involved in business and entrepreneurship, which is fostering innovation, job creation, and economic growth. We can realize the full potential of female entrepreneurs and build a more affluent and inclusive future for all by recognizing their accomplishments, tackling their obstacles, and giving them the assistance they require to be successful.

Chapter 3

Innovators in Science and Technology

In any account of the advancement of humanity, one must recognize the important contributions made by women in STEM areas (science, technology, engineering, and mathematics). The recognition of women's accomplishments in these fields has frequently been marginalized or disregarded, despite their critical roles in influencing our perception of the world and spurring innovation. This chapter looks at ways to support gender diversity and inclusiveness in STEM fields, highlights the groundbreaking discoveries made by women, and examines the many aspects of the challenges that they encounter.

Women have made major contributions to the growth of science and technology throughout history, from the ancient philosophers to the modern visionaries. Their achievements have pushed the frontiers of human knowledge and creativity, in addition to advancing scientific inquiry beyond disciplinary boundaries. The important contributions that women make to scientific and technical breakthroughs have, however, been frequently overlooked in favor of male characters in these tales.

By recognizing the outstanding and varied contributions made by women in STEM, we want to rectify this historical omission through our inquiry. We explore the tales of trailblazers who succeeded in pursuing their passions and leaving a lasting legacy in their areas despite social pressures and systemic barriers. From the ancient scholar Hypatia of Alexandria to contemporary visionaries like Jane Goodall, the history of women in STEM is filled with motivational stories of perseverance, ingenuity, and strength.

We also face the stark realities of gender inequality and discrimination, which continue to impede women's advancement and full involvement in STEM fields. We draw attention to the difficulties that women encounter, which range from institutional prejudices and stereotyping to uneven access to opportunities and resources. We believe that by highlighting these difficulties, we might contribute to a better understanding of the difficulties in reaching gender parity in STEM.

Stories of triumph and resiliency among these challenges give hope and motivate change. We celebrate the accomplishments of women who have defied expectations, torn down boundaries and emerged as trailblazers and powerful figures in their fields. The potential and possibilities available to women in STEM disciplines are highlighted by their experiences.

The programs and tactics used to support and empower women in STEM education and jobs are also examined. It is through these initiatives—which range from mentorship programs to advocacy groups—that women may flourish and create a welcoming atmosphere.

This chapter provides evidence of the persistence and unyielding will of women in STEM fields. Beyond only honoring their accomplishments, it also acts as a call to action to eliminate structural inequities and a pledge to build a future in which every person, regardless of gender, has an equal chance to contribute to and profit from the wonders of science and technology.

In Chapter Five, we shift our attention to the world of cultural icons and creative visionaries. In addition, women have had a revolutionary impact on trends, narratives, and aesthetics in the media, entertainment, and arts sectors. In the upcoming chapter, we will examine how female cultural idols influence public perception and dispel preconceptions, as well as the possibilities and problems faced by women in the creative sectors and the vital role they play in advancing diversity and inclusion in cultural settings. Join us as we honor the fortitude, ingenuity, and tenacity of women who are transforming and enhancing our cultural landscapes.

Contributions of Women to STEM Fields

In the history of science, technology, engineering, and mathematics (STEM), women have been key figures in invention and knowledge. From prehistoric times to the present, their efforts have played a critical role in forming our perception of reality and advancing numerous academic fields. This section honors the diverse and significant achievements made by women in STEM, highlighting how important it is to recognize and appreciate them.

Early innovators and ancient scholars

Women were essential to the advancement of knowledge and science even in ancient times. Ancient academics disobeyed social conventions to investigate the secrets of the natural world and the mysteries of the universe, from the astronomical discoveries of Aglaonike to the mathematical prowess of Hypatia of Alexandria. By laying the groundwork for upcoming generations of mathematicians and scientists, their groundbreaking work also established a standard for women's participation in STEM professions.

Mediaeval and Renaissance trailblazers

Women continued to leave their lasting imprints on STEM subjects throughout the Middle Ages and the Renaissance, despite strong social hurdles. The polymathic abbess Hildegard of Bingen was one of the notable figures in natural history, medicine, and music composition. Through her publications on herbalism and therapeutic plants, Hildegard demonstrated her in-depth knowledge of pharmacology and botany, which advanced medical science in her day.

Enlightenment and Industrial Revolution Innovators

Women were at the vanguard of ground-breaking discoveries during the Enlightenment and Industrial Revolutions, which saw a rise in scientific research and technical invention. People such as the English paleontologist Mary Anning transformed our knowledge of life in the prehistoric era by finding fossils along the Jurassic Coast. By dispelling then-current scientific beliefs, Anning's meticulous digs and fossil specimens shed light on early ecosystems and evolutionary biology.

Modern-day Pioneers and Innovators

Women have been at the forefront of groundbreaking advances in science and technology in the contemporary age, having made significant progress in STEM subjects. Pioneering scientist and chemist Marie Curie, for example, was the first woman to win the Nobel Prize for her unmatched contributions to the field of radioactive research. Scientific research was revolutionized by Curie's pioneering work, which set the stage for developments in nuclear physics and medical imaging.

Contemporary Visionaries and Leaders

Women are now leaders and visionaries in STEM fields, propelling innovation and influencing the direction of science and technology. The study and protection of endangered animals have devoted the lives of notable individuals such as Jane Goodall, the renowned primatologist and conservationist. Many advances in primatology and wildlife conservation have resulted from Goodall's groundbreaking studies on chimpanzee behavior and conservation initiatives, which have motivated future generations to support environmental stewardship.

Emphasizing Recognition and Appreciation

The contributions made by women in STEM professions are many, significant, and worthy of praise. We respect the contributions made by women throughout history, encourage the next generation, and open the door for a more diverse and equitable scientific community when we recognize their accomplishments. It is critical to acknowledge the essential work that women do in STEM fields and to make sure that future generations will remember and honor their achievements. We can develop a culture that supports diversity, equity, and achievement in STEM professions by expressing gratitude and acknowledgment to one another.

Groundbreaking discoveries and advancements

Throughout human history, women have played a pivotal role in numerous revolutionary discoveries and technological advancements. Women have been essential in driving scientific advancement and technological innovation, from solving the secrets of the cosmos to transforming how we engage with technology. This section explores the outstanding accomplishments of women in STEM, emphasizing their resourcefulness, tenacity, and long-lasting influence on society.

Unraveling the Mysteries of Life:

The identification of DNA's structure—the blueprint for life itself—was one of the greatest scientific discoveries ever made. Rosalind Franklin was an English scientist and X-ray crystallographer whose groundbreaking work in X-ray diffraction helped to clarify the double-helix structure of DNA. James Watson and Francis Crick's ensuing model of the DNA molecule was made possible by Franklin's ground-breaking photographs, which offered vital insights into the molecular structure of DNA. Franklin's efforts continue to be crucial to our comprehension of genetics and molecular biology, even though he faced many challenges and was overlooked for the Nobel Prize given for this discovery.

Innovation and Groundbreaking Findings Produced by Female Technologists and Scientists

Within computer science and technology, women have played a pivotal role in propelling innovation and molding the digital terrain. The foundation for contemporary computing was laid by Ada Lovelace, who is frequently credited as the first computer programmer in history. She developed the algorithms for Charles Babbage's Analytical Engine in the 1800s. Lovelace's prescient observations on the possibilities of computers implied the next century's digital revolution that would completely change society.

Breaking Barriers in Space Exploration

Another field in which women have broken down barriers and made important contributions is space exploration. In 1963, Soviet cosmonaut Valentina Tereshkova made history by becoming the first female astronaut to launch the Vostok 6 spacecraft. A major turning point in the history of space exploration was reached by Tereshkova's groundbreaking expedition, which opened the door for later generations of female astronauts and cosmonauts to travel beyond Earth's boundaries.

Revolutionizing Medicine and Healthcare

Women have also made significant contributions to the medical and healthcare revolutions through their groundbreaking discoveries and inventions. During the Crimean War, Florence Nightingale, who is frequently cited as the founder of modern nursing, transformed healthcare delivery by introducing evidence-based approaches. By emphasizing cleanliness, hygiene, and statistical analysis, Florence Nightingale saved many lives and elevated the nursing profession.

Empowering Communities Through Environmental Science

When it comes to understanding and addressing urgent environmental concerns, women have led the way in environmental research. A worldwide environmental movement was initiated by American marine biologist and conservationist Rachel Carson's groundbreaking study, "Silent Spring," which revealed the harmful effects of pesticides on ecosystems and human health. Because of Carson's ground-breaking book, lawmakers are now more conscious than ever of the need to preserve the environment for future generations and to take immediate action.

Honoring Legacies and Inspiring Future Generations

The world we live in today and the path of human history have been drastically altered by the ground-breaking discoveries and breakthroughs achieved by women in STEM professions. Women in STEM fields have boundless potential, as evidenced by their inventiveness, tenacity, and steadfast commitment to scientific research. To ensure that the history of invention and discovery endure for many more years, let us endeavor to encourage future generations of women to seek careers in science, technology, engineering, and mathematics as we celebrate their accomplishments and pay tribute to their legacies.

Obstacles that Women in STEM Encounter and Tactics to Advance Gender Diversity

Despite their outstanding accomplishments and contributions to STEM disciplines, women still face numerous obstacles that prevent them from fully participating in and advancing in these fields. For women seeking professions in science, technology, engineering, and mathematics, structural impediments, gender bias, and unequal opportunities continue to pose significant challenges. This section looks at the various obstacles that women in STEM encounter and looks at ways to encourage gender diversity and create more welcoming environments.

Gender Bias and Stereotypes

Gender bias and preconceptions are among the most prevalent obstacles that women in STEM must overcome. These can take many different forms, including implicit biases, microaggressions, and blatant discrimination. Girls are frequently dissuaded from pursuing STEM fields from an early age because of societal assumptions and prejudices that link these fields to masculinity and natural aptitude. These prejudices may affect a person's educational and professional decisions, which may result in unequal opportunities and representation for women in STEM fields.

Unequal Opportunities and Access to Resources

In addition, women in STEM face discrimination and restricted access to resources such as financing, opportunities for professional growth, and mentorship. Studies have indicated that women are not as likely as men to be awarded research funding, which restricts their capacity to take on large-scale research projects and grow in their professions. Access to networking and mentoring opportunities, which are essential for career growth and success in STEM professions, may also present challenges for women.

Work-life balance and family responsibilities

Women in STEM have a lot of challenges when it comes to juggling work and family obligations, especially those in academic and research-intensive fields. The long hours, frequent travel, and publishing pressure that come with a STEM profession might conflict with traditional gender roles and caregiving obligations. Women may experience discrimination and stigma for taking maternity leave or asking for flexible work schedules, or they may feel pressured to put family before career progress.

Lack of representation and visibility

The underrepresentation of women in STEM organizations and institutions' leadership and decision-making roles is another barrier to gender diversity and inclusivity. Women in STEM fields may find it difficult to advance in their careers and to dispel negative assumptions about their aptitude for leadership positions due to a lack of visible role models and mentors. Innovation and creativity in the STEM sector may also be hampered by a lack of different viewpoints and experiences in STEM leadership.

Strategies for Promoting Gender Diversity and Inclusion

To solve the obstacles that women in STEM encounter, there needs to be a concentrated effort made to advance gender diversity and foster more welcoming settings. Implementing practices and regulations that lessen prejudice and discrimination, encouraging inclusive hiring and promotion procedures, and offering assistance and resources to women at all phases of their STEM careers are some strategies for boosting gender diversity. In addition to providing support for women in STEM fields, mentoring programs, networking events, and work-life balance campaigns can also help cultivate an inclusive and equitable culture.

Even though there are many obstacles for women in STEM, they also have resiliency, tenacity, and a love of learning that propel advancement and creativity. We can realize the full potential of women in STEM and make sure that their contributions are appreciated, acknowledged, and celebrated by eliminating systemic hurdles, fostering gender diversity, and building more inclusive settings. Working together, we can create a future in which everyone, regardless of gender, has equal access to chances to pursue their passions and make contributions to the fields of science, technology, engineering, and math.

Women's Accomplishments STEM

Many women have overcome obstacles and excelled in STEM disciplines, setting an example and laying the path for upcoming generations of scientists, engineers, and innovators. Their tales serve as a tribute to tenacity, fortitude, and the transformational potential of ardor and willpower. This section honors these trailblazers' victories and efforts, highlighting their incredible moves and the contributions they have made to the fields of science, technology, engineering, and mathematics.

Marie Curie: Pioneering Researcher and Nobel Laureate

One of the most famous people in scientific history, Marie Curie is well known for her revolutionary studies on radioactivity and for being the first woman to receive the Nobel Prize. Curie's discoveries, which included isolating polonium and radium, transformed our knowledge of atomic physics and paved the way for developments in cancer treatment and imaging. Curie's unrelenting dedication to scientific inquiry and her relentless pursuit of knowledge garnered her international fame and secured her status as a pioneer in STEM while overcoming enormous hurdles and discrimination as a woman in a sector dominated by men.

Katherine Johnson: Trailblazing Mathematician and Space Pioneer

NASA's Mercury and Apollo space missions were made possible in large part by the calculations made by the innovative mathematician and space pioneer Katherine Johnson. Johnson overcame institutional racism and discrimination as an African American woman working in segregated NASA facilities to rise to the position of highly esteemed mathematician within the organization. Admired as a hidden force behind some of NASA's greatest accomplishments, her accurate estimates of orbital trajectories and flight routes were crucial in guaranteeing the safety and success of astronauts.

Grace Hopper: Computer Scientist and Programming Pioneer

Grace Hopper changed the way humans engage with technology by developing computer programming languages, which led to her making ground-breaking contributions to the fields of computer science and software engineering. Hopper, a mathematician and naval officer, created the first compiler for a programming language, setting the stage for contemporary software development and computer programming. Her contributions, which included creating the widely used programming language COBOL, changed computing and sparked the digital revolution. This earned her the moniker "Amazing Grace" and solidified her reputation as a trailblazer in STEM.

Mae Jemison: Astronaut and Space Explorer

Being the first African American woman in space, Mae Jemison broke down barriers and inspired countless people with her groundbreaking accomplishments in space exploration. Jemison broke preconceptions and disregarded expectations as a NASA astronaut, engineer, and doctor by daring to travel to the farthest reaches of space on the Space Shuttle Endeavour. Jemison uses her platform to encourage the next generation of explorers and innovators to aim high, even after her historic mission. She also continues to push for STEM education and diversity in the sciences.

Inspiring the Next Generation

Strong reminders of the infinite possibilities and endless potential that await those who dare to dream big and never give up on their quest for knowledge and understanding are provided by the inspiring success stories of women in STEM fields. By recognizing their accomplishments and narrating their experiences, we encourage the upcoming cohort of female STEM professionals to challenge norms, shatter boundaries, and leave their imprint on society. In addition to recognizing the contributions of these trailblazers, let us pledge to expand access to STEM fields for women and to provide equal opportunities for them. Only then will we be able to help every aspiring scientist, engineer, or innovator realize their full potential and make a positive impact on society?

Projects and Activities that Encourage Females to Pursue Careers in STEM

Many initiatives and programs have been launched to promote and empower women in STEM education and jobs, raising awareness of the difficulties experienced by women in the field and the significance of encouraging gender diversity and inclusion. These initiatives, which range from advocacy groups to mentorship programs, are essential to creating a positive environment in which women can succeed. In addition to discussing their effects on advancing gender diversity and empowering women in the profession, this section examines some of the major projects and programs that assist women in STEM.

Mentorship Programs

Mentorship programs provide women in STEM fields with vital assistance and direction, as well as chances for professional growth, skill development, and networking. Experienced professionals may help women navigate the obstacles of STEM jobs by sharing insights, offering guidance, and encouraging them one-on-one through mentoring relationships. Mentorship programs enable women in STEM to overcome barriers and realize their goals by boosting their self-esteem, growing their professional networks, and creating a sense of community.

Advocacy Organizations

Advocacy organizations are essential in promoting gender diversity and inclusion policies and practices, as well as the interests of women in STEM fields. These groups seek to eliminate structural barriers by offering resources and assistance, advocating for equitable opportunities and representation, and increasing public awareness of the difficulties experienced by women in STEM fields. Advocacy organizations help to create more fair and welcoming conditions for women in STEM by elevating the voices of women in the field and pushing for institutional and societal change.

Professional development workshops and training

Professional development seminars and training programs provide women in STEM fields with chances to grow professionally, learn new things, and improve their skills. Tailored to the unique requirements and interests of women in STEM, these programs cover a wide range of topics, including technical training, communication skills development, and leadership development. Women can bolster their skills, become more competitive in the job market, and explore chances for career growth and advancement by making investments in their professional development.

STEM Education Initiatives for Girls

Through the provision of educational resources, mentorship opportunities, and experiential learning opportunities, STEM education initiatives for girls seek to empower and inspire the upcoming generation of women in STEM fields. These programs aim to break down barriers and preconceptions that can deter girls from participating in STEM fields while also fostering their enthusiasm and confidence in these fields from an early age. These programs seek to develop a pipeline of gifted and diverse people who are prepared to pursue professions in STEM fields and fuel future creativity and discovery by supporting STEM education for girls.

Empowering women in STEM

The campaigns and programs that encourage women in STEM are essential to building more diverse, equitable, and inclusive workplaces where women can prosper. These programs enable women to break through barriers, follow their passions, and make significant contributions to STEM fields by offering mentorship, advocacy, professional development, and educational opportunities.

By continuing to assist women in STEM fields, we not only help people reach their full potential but also promote innovation, advancement, and prosperity for society at large.

Although they have been instrumental in reshaping science and technology, women still encounter challenges in their quest for achievement. We can build a more diverse and inclusive scientific community by acknowledging their accomplishments, removing obstacles to gender parity, and backing programs that uplift women in STEM. We can guarantee that women will prosper and continue to contribute significantly to the fields of science and technology by working together.

Chapter 4

Voices in Politics and Advocacy

Historically, women have been integral to the advancement of social change, the defense of human rights, and the shaping of public policy in the advocacy and political spheres. Women persevere in assuming leadership positions and fighting for issues that impact both their local communities and society at large, despite the many challenges they confront.

Addressing the structural obstacles that women face, such as discrimination, gender prejudice, and underrepresentation, is crucial to comprehending the influence of women in activism and politics. Historically, women's contributions have been marginalized, and these challenges have their roots in those traditions. However, women have shown the transformational potential of female leadership through their tenacity and fortitude, which have not only allowed them to pave the way in various fields.

It is impossible to understand the current state of women's activism and politics without taking into account the historical economic exploitation of the Third World. **As discussed in Chapter Two**, colonization had lasting effects on many nations' economic systems, resulting in circumstances that still affect social and political dynamics today. Modern female leaders and activists work against a backdrop of puzzled indigenous livelihoods and the legacy of extractive industries.

For example, in many regions of Africa, Asia, and Latin America, the systematic injustices established during the colonial era continue to influence women's political activity. Due to these historical injustices, there has been a push for women to take the lead in reclaiming positions of influence and power to right historical wrongs and create equitable communities.

This chapter explores the many tactics women have used to get beyond these structural obstacles and bring about significant change. Women are making significant progress in a variety of fields, including community structuring, grassroots movements, and positions in government and international organizations. The accounts of these women not only highlight their outstanding accomplishments but also shed light on the creative strategies they used to negotiate and alter their political environments.

We may better appreciate the complex roles that women play in public life by looking at the interactions between past economic exploitation and modern political activism.

Moving forward, we will look into the complex connections between these political and legislative endeavors and larger social justice movements, particularly concerning addressing the cultural legacy of colonialism. This interdependence emphasizes how important it is to tackle decolonization and marginalized populations' empowerment from a comprehensive standpoint. Come explore the economic aspects of colonialism and its legacy with us in the upcoming chapter, which will provide the groundwork for comprehending the all-encompassing tactics required to promote genuine freedom and fairness.

Participation of Women in Government and Politics

One important measure of gender equality and democratic governance is the presence of women in politics and the government. Though there has been a noticeable increase in the number of women participating in political processes globally in recent decades, there are still large gaps and persistent underrepresentation of women in elected seats and positions of decision-making. This section explores the current state of women's representation in political institutions, the variables affecting women's political engagement, and the significance of gender diversity in governance for democratic governance and efficient policymaking.

Status of Women's Representation

Women still make up less than half of the world's population, but they are still underrepresented in political institutions everywhere. Women only hold 25.5% of seats in national parliaments worldwide as of 2021, according to the Inter-Parliamentary Union. This is a slight rise from prior years but still falls well short of gender parity. Women also continue to be underrepresented in executive leadership roles and ministerial positions; they make up a very small percentage of heads of state and government.

Factors Influencing Women's Participation in Politics

Systemic discrimination, structural hurdles, and cultural and societal norms all play a part in the underrepresentation of women in government and politics. Women are frequently discouraged from pursuing political careers by gender stereotypes and bigotry, and their participation is further hampered by institutional obstacles such as unequal access to resources, inadequate financial assistance, and deeply ingrained power networks. Inequalities in representation can be sustained by discriminatory political party structures and election systems that offer obstacles for women aspiring to the political sphere.

The importance of gender diversity in governance

To make sure that women's viewpoints, experiences, and interests are fairly represented in decision-making processes, gender diversity in governance is crucial. Research indicates that enhanced gender diversity in political institutions promotes more inclusive policymaking, raises awareness of concerns unique to women, and improves governance. Gender-balanced institutions are better suited to address the complex issues facing society and advance social justice, equity, and human rights for all citizens by embracing a variety of perspectives and points of view.

Promoting Women's Political Participation

A variety of tactics, such as legislative actions, electoral reforms, affirmative action programs, and focused capacity-building projects, are used in the pursuit of advancing women's political representation and engagement. The implementation of quotas and electoral gender quotas has demonstrated efficacy in augmenting the participation of women in political establishments.

This mechanism is vital in surmounting structural obstacles and propelling gender equality in the realm of governance. To further empower women to engage and succeed in politics, it is imperative to address institutional and cultural prejudices, invest in women's leadership development, and offer mentorship and support networks.

Not only is the presence of women in politics and governance a question of fairness and equality, but it is also necessary for democratic systems to work well. We can develop more inclusive and responsive political institutions that better represent the varied needs and ambitions of all citizens by tackling the structural obstacles and systematic disparities that prevent women from entering the political sphere. Let us keep pushing for laws and procedures that support women's empowerment, elevate the voices of women, and create a more inclusive and equitable political environment for coming generations as we work toward gender parity in government.

Influence of Female Activists and Leaders on Human Rights and Social Justice

Promoting racial justice, gender equality, and several other important concerns, female leaders and activists have been at the vanguard of social justice movements. Their contributions have played a crucial role in influencing legislative changes, posing problems with structural inequities, and promoting inclusive communities. To honor the tremendous contributions made by women to the fields of social justice and human rights, this section will focus on their fortitude, bravery, and unshakable dedication to bringing about constructive change.

Advancing Gender Equality

In addition to opposing discriminatory laws and practices and advancing gender-sensitive policies, female leaders and activists have played a critical role in advancing gender equality and women's rights. Prominent figures like Nobel laureate and education activist Malala Yousafzai have dedicated their lives to advocating for girls' education, questioning patriarchal traditions, and enabling young ladies to follow their dreams. To advance women's rights and gender equality, grassroots activists and community organizers have also fought to address issues including economic inequality, gender-based violence, and reproductive rights. They have done this by promoting legislative changes and societal transformation.

Promoting Racial Justice and Equity

Women of color have been essential in the advancement of racial justice and equity, having led the charge to abolish racial discrimination, police brutality, and structural racism. Prominent figures like civil rights activist and academic Angela Davis have been vocal proponents of racial justice, contesting systemic racism and pushing for revolutionary transformation. Black women-led movements, including the Black Lives Matter movement, have brought attention to the intersectionality of oppression, fought for the rights and dignity of marginalized people, and mobilized communities and protestors while demanding accountability for racial injustices.

Fostering inclusive societies

Women have made significant contributions to the development of inclusive societies that value variety, encourage tolerance, and uphold all people's right to human rights. Leaders that have steered their nations towards stability and advancement include Ellen Johnson Sirleaf, the first female president of Liberia and recipient of the Nobel Peace Prize. She has championed peacebuilding, reconciliation, and human rights. To foster solidarity and social cohesion in various countries, grassroots activists and community organizers have fought against xenophobia, religious intolerance, and other types of prejudice.

A Legacy of Resilience and Courage

The lasting and significant influence that female leaders and activists have had on social justice and human rights is a testament to their tenacity, bravery, and will to bring about constructive change. Generations have been motivated to fight for justice and equality by their contributions, which have changed societies and upended long-standing injustices. Let's continue to elevate the voices of women leaders and activists as we commemorate their accomplishments and pay tribute to their legacies, acknowledging their crucial role in creating a fairer, inclusive, and just society for all.

Challenges Faced by Women in Politics and Activism

Numerous obstacles prevent women from entering politics and advocating for themselves, which limits their ability to lead and participate in public life. These problems are caused by institutionalized discrimination, deeply rooted gender biases, and discriminatory behaviors that continue to exist in social and political organizations. To create political systems that are more inclusive and egalitarian, it is imperative to recognize and solve these challenges.

Gender Bias and Stereotypes

Gender bias and preconceptions are major obstacles for women working in politics and advocacy. Women are frequently scrutinized because of their perceived leadership potential, manners, and outward looks. Preconceived notions about women's capacity for emotional stability, leadership, and expertise in fields like economic policy and national security can damage their reputations and impede their advancement in the political sphere. Media coverage demonstrates gender bias as well, with female politicians receiving more attention and a more unfavorable image than their male colleagues.

Discrimination and harassment

Sexual discrimination, verbal abuse, and internet harassment are just a few of the many forms of discrimination and harassment that women in politics and advocacy are susceptible to. Threats of violence, hostile surroundings, and intimidation are all possible for female politicians and activists, especially when they are standing up for divisive or controversial causes.

Women's safety and well-being are compromised by such behavior, which also prevents them from fully engaging in political processes and exercising their rights to free speech and political participation.

Systemic Barriers to Leadership

Women's leadership in politics and advocacy is severely hampered by structural hurdles found in political institutions and party systems. Limited access to capital, networks for fundraising, and campaign infrastructure can work against female candidates, making it more difficult for them to run a strong campaign. Furthermore, women find it difficult to obtain leadership positions and decision-making roles inside political parties and government institutions due to closed political networks and deeply ingrained power structures that frequently favor incumbent male politicians.

Intersectional Challenges

The complex interplay of discrimination and marginalization based on race, ethnicity, class, sexual orientation, and disability further complicates women's experiences in politics and advocacy. When it comes to navigating political processes and speaking up for their interests, women from marginalized or underrepresented areas confront particular difficulties in addition to heightened barriers. Their access to opportunities, resources, and leadership roles may be restricted by intersectional discrimination and bias, which can exacerbate existing political disparities and undermine attempts to promote social justice and gender parity.

Strategies for Overcoming Challenges

To effectively address the obstacles that women encounter in politics and advocacy, a multidisciplinary strategy that tackles both individual and institutional barriers is needed. The implementation of laws and policies that uphold women's rights and gender equality, the development of an inclusive and respectful political culture, the provision of assistance and training to female candidates and activists, and the amplification of the voices of marginalized women through intersectional advocacy and coalition-building are some strategies for overcoming these obstacles. We can create conditions where women may fully engage, lead, and contribute to determining the future of our society by tearing down systemic barriers and promoting more inclusive and equitable political institutions.

Success Stories of Women Using Advocacy and Political Engagement to Drive Change

Women have always been at the vanguard of political activity and advocacy, spearheading social change movements and advancing important causes. Their tales encourage optimism, fortitude, and a resolve to bring about constructive change both inside and outside of their communities. The amazing success stories of women who have impacted legislative decisions, organized grassroots movements, and galvanized communities to confront urgent social, economic, and environmental issues are highlighted in this section.

Malala Yousafzai: Education Activist

Malala Yousafzai's storyline is one of bravery, tenacity, and an unshakable commitment to female equality and education. Malala, who was raised in the Swat Valley of Pakistan, disobeyed the Taliban's prohibition on girls attending school and went on to become a vocal supporter of girls' education rights. Malala persisted in speaking up despite threats and acts of violence, telling her tale to the world and encouraging millions of people to support her cause. Malala's advocacy work earned her the distinction of becoming the youngest-ever Nobel Peace Prize recipient in 2014, which helped spread her message and inspire support for girls' education around the world.

Tarana Burke: Founder of the #MeToo Movement

The #MeToo movement, started by Tarana Burke, forced a worldwide conversation about sexual harassment and assault and gave survivors the confidence to speak up and seek justice for their stories. Burke, a victim of sexual assault herself, started the #MeToo movement in 2006 intending to support and unite survivors—especially women of color and members of marginalized groups. After going viral on social media in 2017, the campaign attracted a lot of attention and momentum, revealing the widespread prevalence of sexual misconduct in a variety of professions and igniting a wave of revelations. To prevent sexual violence and harassment, Burke's work has changed the way that people talk about consent, power relations, and accountability. This has resulted in legislative changes and cultural transformations.

Greta Thunberg: Climate Activist

Millions of young people have been inspired by Greta Thunberg's brave call for climate action to come to the streets and demand immediate action to address the issue. At the age of fifteen, Thunberg began missing school to stage protests outside the Swedish parliament, where she advocated for more environmental protection and stricter climate laws. Students throughout the world joined her "Fridays for Future" strikes to demand climate justice and hold governments responsible for their inaction, starting a worldwide youth movement inspired by her lone protest.

Being a major voice in the battle against climate change, Thunberg has mobilized public support and forced governments to prioritize environmental sustainability through her impassioned speeches at international forums and her unwavering stance on climate action.

Stacey Abrams: Voting Rights Activist

American democracy has greatly benefited from Stacey Abrams' ceaseless efforts to increase voting rights and fight voter suppression. Abrams, who founded Fair Fight Action, has spearheaded initiatives to defend voting rights, boost voter turnout, and counteract strategies of intimidation that target communities of color and marginalized populations. To gain historic victories and change the political landscape, her advocacy was crucial in energizing voters during Georgia's runoff elections and the 2020 presidential election. Abrams' dedication to social justice and democracy serves as an inspiration to activists and organizers nationwide, highlighting the significance of community involvement and grassroots organizing in creating a society that is more inclusive and equal.

Inspiring Change and Empowering Communities

The inspiring stories of women bringing about change via political involvement and campaigning show the transformational potential of grassroots movements, group efforts, and unrelenting dedication to social justice issues. Across a range of issues, including voting rights, climate action, and education, these women have demonstrated that regular people can have a remarkable influence when they band together to demand change. Let us be motivated to make the world a better place for everyone by their bravery, resiliency, and tenacity as we celebrate their accomplishments and pay tribute to their legacies.

Strategies for Increasing Women's Participation and Leadership in Public Life

Gender equality, inclusive governance, and democratic representation all depend on increasing the involvement and leadership of women in public life. Proactive actions and creative thinking are required to remove the obstacles preventing women from participating in political processes and decision-making. A variety of strategies and best practices, such as quotas, affirmative action laws, leadership development efforts, and mentoring programs, are examined in this section to encourage women's political leadership and participation.

Gender Quotas and Affirmative Action Policies

Legislative initiatives aimed at increasing the presence of women in political institutions and decision-making bodies include affirmative action programs and gender quotas. Legislative, party, and electoral quotas are only a few examples of the different shapes quotas can take. They might also involve reserved seats or demands for a gender balance on candidate lists. Quotas can guarantee women's participation in political processes and help to break down systemic obstacles by imposing a minimum level of female representation. This helps to create more varied and representative government systems.

Leadership development programs

Programs for developing leadership abilities give women the tools, connections, and support systems they need to pursue and succeed in careers in politics. These courses could cover topics like networking, policy analysis, public speaking, campaign management, and networking, giving women the skills and self-assurance they need to succeed in political settings and pursue their goals of becoming leaders. Organizations and institutions may create a pipeline of competent women leaders and promote a more inclusive and diverse political landscape by investing in women's leadership development.

Mentorship and sponsorship initiatives

Experienced leaders and young female politicians and activists are paired through mentoring and sponsorship programs, which offer opportunities for career progression, support, and direction. Mentors help mentees manage political obstacles, create networks, and hone their leadership abilities by providing guidance, support, and experience. By using their connections and influence to support and encourage their protégés' professional growth, sponsors provide doors for women to pursue leadership and decision-making positions. Organizations can help women break through obstacles and realize their full potential in public life by providing mentorship and sponsorship opportunities.

Promoting Gender-Responsive Policies and Practices

To create inclusive and equitable political settings that encourage women's leadership and participation, gender-responsive policies and practices must be promoted. This entails establishing policies to combat harassment and violence against women, guaranteeing equal access to opportunities and resources, and incorporating gender viewpoints into the development of policies and the decision-making process. Policymakers can foster more conducive and empowering conditions for women's political engagement and empowerment by including gender issues in political agendas and governance systems.

Building Coalitions and Alliances

For women to advance in politics and hold leadership positions, they must form coalitions and alliances with other stakeholders from all sectors. Women's organizations, civil society organizations, political parties, and government agencies can all work together to strengthen their collective voice and push for institutional and policy changes that support women's empowerment and gender equality. Coalitions give the movement for gender-inclusive democracy and governance a platform for resource sharing, campaign coordination, and mobilizing support for women's rights and interests.

Empowering Women's Political Engagement

To increase women's leadership and participation in public life, a comprehensive and multidimensional strategy that addresses institutional reforms removes structural hurdles, and creates an atmosphere that is encouraging and supportive of women's political engagement is needed. Stakeholders may give women the chance to contribute their views, perspectives, and leadership abilities to the decision-making processes that define our societies by putting creative methods into practice and enacting gender-responsive policies. As we endeavor to attain gender parity and inclusive governance, let us persist in advocating for the entitlements and portrayal of women in public life, guaranteeing that their opinions are acknowledged and their input is esteemed in shaping the destiny of our societies and countries.

Empowering Women's Voices in Politics and Advocacy

To create more inclusive, egalitarian, and democratic societies, women's voices in politics and activism are crucial. By elevating the voices of women, tackling structural challenges, and advocating for women's political empowerment, we can fully use the potential of fifty percent of the population to tackle the most critical issues confronting our planet. Let us reaffirm our commitment to furthering gender equality and making sure that women's opinions are heard and valued in determining the future of our communities and countries as we honor the accomplishments and tenacity of women in politics and advocacy.

Chapter 5

Cultural Icons and Creative Visionaries

In the realm of arts, entertainment, and media, women have long been influential figures, breaking boundaries, challenging norms, and shaping cultural landscapes. From trailblazing actresses and musicians to visionary writers and visual artists, female cultural icons have left an indelible mark on society, shaping perceptions, challenging stereotypes, and inspiring generations. This chapter celebrates the contributions of women in creative industries, explores their impact on shaping cultural narratives, and examines the challenges and opportunities they face in navigating these spaces. Additionally, it highlights the pivotal role of women in promoting diversity, equity, and inclusion in cultural spheres.

Influence of Women in the Arts, Entertainment, and Media Industries

Women have exerted a profound influence on the arts, entertainment, and media industries, leaving an indelible mark on cultural narratives, aesthetics, and creative expressions. Their contributions span various domains, including acting, music, writing, visual arts, and beyond, shaping trends, challenging conventions, and amplifying diverse voices. This section delves into the multifaceted and dynamic influence of women in these fields, exploring their evolving roles as creators, innovators, and leaders in cultural production.

Acting: Redefining Roles and Representation

In the realm of acting, women have redefined roles and representation, challenging stereotypes and expanding the scope of narratives. From trailblazers like Katharine Hepburn and Meryl Streep to contemporary icons like Viola Davis and Lupita Nyong'o, female actors have brought depth, complexity, and authenticity to their portrayals, pushing boundaries and challenging norms. Their performances have not only entertained audiences but also sparked important conversations about gender, identity, and power dynamics in society.

Music: Shaping Sounds and Identities

In the music industry, women have been instrumental in shaping sounds and identities, breaking barriers, and pioneering new genres. From jazz legends like Billie Holiday and Ella Fitzgerald to pop icons like Madonna and Beyoncé, women musicians have wielded their voices and talents to captivate audiences, challenge conventions, and inspire movements for social change. Their music has served as a soundtrack to cultural movements, expressing resilience, empowerment, and solidarity across generations.

Writing: Crafting Stories and Perspectives

Women writers have crafted stories and perspectives that resonate with audiences, illuminating diverse experiences and challenging dominant narratives. From literary giants like Virginia Woolf and Toni Morrison to contemporary voices like Chimamanda Ngozi Adichie and J.K. Rowling, women authors have enriched literary landscapes with their imagination, insight, and creativity. Their works explore themes of identity, agency, and belonging, inviting readers to empathize with characters and worlds that reflect the complexity of human existence.

Visual Arts: Expressing Vision and Meaning

In the realm of the visual arts, women have expressed vision and meaning through their creations, pushing boundaries and challenging perceptions. From Renaissance painters like Artemisia Gentileschi and Sofonisba Anguissola to contemporary artists like Yayoi Kusama and Cindy Sherman, women visual artists have employed diverse mediums and styles to explore themes of identity, politics, and social justice. Their artworks provoke thought, evoke emotion, and inspire dialogue, inviting viewers to reconsider their perspectives and engage with pressing issues of our time.

Media: Shaping Discourse and Representation

Women in media have played a pivotal role in shaping discourse and representation, amplifying diverse voices and perspectives in the public sphere. From pioneering journalists like Nellie Bly and Ida B. Wells to contemporary media moguls like Oprah Winfrey and Shonda Rhimes, women media professionals have challenged biases, exposed injustices, and championed stories that resonate with audiences. Their work has expanded the boundaries of journalism, entertainment, and storytelling, fostering a more inclusive and equitable media landscape.

Celebrating Women's Creative Contributions

The influence of women in the arts, entertainment, and media industries is as diverse and expansive as the creative expressions they produce. From redefining roles and representation to shaping cultural narratives and fostering creative expression, women have made invaluable contributions to these fields, enriching our cultural landscapes and inspiring generations with their talent, vision, and resilience. As we celebrate their achievements and honor their legacies, let us continue to champion the rights and representation of women in the arts, entertainment, and media, ensuring that their voices are heard and their contributions are recognized and celebrated in shaping the cultural narratives of our time.

Trailblazing Actresses, Musicians, Writers, and Visual Artists

Throughout history, women have emerged as trailblazers in the arts and creative industries, defying norms, challenging conventions, and paving the way for future generations. This section pays tribute to the pioneering actresses, musicians, writers, and visual artists who have left an indelible mark on cultural landscapes and inspired audiences with their talent, vision, and courage. From the early days of cinema to the contemporary art scene, these women have shattered barriers, pushed boundaries, and redefined artistic expression.

Trailblazing Actresses: Defying Expectations on Screen

Actresses have long been at the forefront of cultural change, using their platforms to challenge stereotypes and advocate for social progress. Pioneers like Mary Pickford and Katharine Hepburn defied societal norms and blazed trails for future generations of actresses. Icons such as Audrey Hepburn and Hattie McDaniel broke racial barriers, while contemporary stars like Meryl Streep and Viola Davis continue to push boundaries with their diverse and nuanced portrayals. These trailblazing actresses have not only entertained audiences but also empowered them with their authenticity, resilience, and commitment to excellence.

Visionary Musicians: Transforming Sounds and Identities

Musicians have played a crucial role in shaping cultural identities and challenging norms through their artistry and innovation. From jazz legends like Billie Holiday and Ella Fitzgerald to rock pioneers like Janis Joplin and Joni Mitchell, female musicians have pushed boundaries and redefined genres. Icons like Aretha Franklin and Madonna have used their music to advocate for social justice and female empowerment, while contemporary artists like Beyoncé and Taylor Swift continue to inspire millions with their creativity and resilience. These visionary musicians have transformed sounds, shattered stereotypes, and empowered listeners with their voices and visions.

Literary Trailblazers: Crafting Stories and Shaping Perspectives

Writers have wielded the power of words to illuminate diverse experiences, challenge dominant narratives, and inspire change. From literary giants like Virginia Woolf and Toni Morrison to contemporary voices like Chimamanda Ngozi Adichie and J.K. Rowling, women writers have captivated readers with their imagination, insight, and storytelling prowess. These literary trailblazers have explored themes of identity, agency, and belonging, inviting readers to engage with complex characters and thought-provoking narratives that reflect the richness of human experience.

Visionary Visual Artists: Expressing Meaning and Vision

Visual artists have used their creativity and vision to provoke thought, evoke emotion, and challenge perceptions through their artworks. From Renaissance painters like Artemisia Gentileschi and Sofonisba Anguissola to contemporary visionaries like Yayoi Kusama and Cindy Sherman, women artists have defied conventions and expanded the boundaries of artistic expression. Their artworks explore themes of identity, politics, and social justice, inviting viewers to reconsider their perspectives and engage with pressing issues of our time.

Conclusion: Honoring the Legacy of Trailblazing Women

The trailblazing actresses, musicians, writers, and visual artists profiled in this section have left an indelible mark on cultural landscapes and inspired generations with their talent, vision, and courage. From defying expectations to pushing boundaries, these women have transformed artistic expression, challenged societal norms, and paved the way for future generations of creators and innovators.

As we celebrate their achievements and honor their legacies, let us continue to champion the rights and representation of women in the arts and creative industries, ensuring that their voices are heard and their contributions are recognized and celebrated for generations to come.

Impact of Female Cultural Icons on Shaping Perceptions and Challenging Stereotypes

Female cultural icons have wielded their influence to challenge stereotypes, redefine norms, and shape cultural narratives, leaving a profound impact on society. This section delves into the transformative influence of iconic figures such as Audrey Hepburn, Nina Simone, Maya Angelou, and Frida Kahlo, exploring how their creative expressions and advocacy efforts have challenged societal norms, amplified marginalized voices, and inspired movements for equality and justice.

Audrey Hepburn: Redefining Elegance and Empathy

Audrey Hepburn, renowned for her grace, elegance, and humanitarian work, transcended the silver screen to become a symbol of compassion and empathy. Through her iconic roles in films like "Breakfast at Tiffany's" and "Roman Holiday," Hepburn challenged conventional notions of beauty and femininity, embracing vulnerability and authenticity. Her philanthropic efforts as a UNICEF Goodwill Ambassador further solidified her legacy as a champion for children's rights and humanitarian causes, inspiring generations to advocate for social justice and global solidarity.

Nina Simone: Using Music as a Vehicle for Social Change

Nina Simone, the "High Priestess of Soul," used her soul-stirring music to confront racism, inequality, and social injustice. Through powerful anthems like "Mississippi Goddam" and "To Be Young, Gifted, and Black," Simone became a voice for the civil rights movement, channeling her experiences as a black woman into songs that spoke truth to power. Her fearless activism and unapologetic artistry challenged societal norms and inspired a generation of activists to fight for racial equality and systemic change.

Maya Angelou: Giving Voice to the Marginalized

Maya Angelou, an acclaimed poet, author, and civil rights activist, used her words to give voice to the marginalized and disenfranchised. Through her groundbreaking memoir, "I Know Why the Caged Bird Sings," Angelou shared her experiences of racism, trauma, and resilience, challenging stereotypes and uplifting the human spirit. As a prominent figure in the civil rights movement, Angelou advocated for equality and justice, using her platform to amplify the voices of black women and inspire social change through storytelling and activism.

Frida Kahlo: Embracing Identity and Resilience through Art

Frida Kahlo, the celebrated Mexican artist, transcended physical and emotional pain through her evocative paintings, challenging societal norms and celebrating her Indigenous heritage. Through self-portraits that depicted her struggles with disability, gender, and identity, Kahlo confronted taboos surrounding women's bodies and redefined beauty on her terms. Her artistry and resilience continue to resonate with audiences worldwide, inspiring women to embrace their identities, express their truths, and find strength in vulnerability.

The Enduring Legacy of Female Cultural Icons

The impact of female cultural icons such as Audrey Hepburn, Nina Simone, Maya Angelou, and Frida Kahlo extends far beyond their artistic achievements. Through their courage, creativity, and advocacy, these women challenged stereotypes, amplified marginalized voices, and inspired movements for equality and justice. As we reflect on their enduring legacies, let us continue to honor their contributions and draw inspiration from their fearless commitment to reshaping cultural narratives and advancing social change.

Opportunities and Challenges Facing Women in the Creative Industries

While women in the creative industries have made significant contributions and achieved remarkable success, they continue to face a myriad of challenges that hinder their advancement. This section delves into the systemic inequalities and structural barriers that impede women's progress in creative fields, including gender bias, unequal representation, and limited access to resources and opportunities. Additionally, it examines the opportunities for empowerment, advocacy, and collective action to address these challenges and foster more inclusive and equitable creative spaces for women.

Gender Bias and Stereotypes in the Creative Industries

Gender bias and stereotypes pervade the creative industries, influencing hiring practices, representation, and opportunities for women. From the perception of women as less competent or creative to the prevalence of gendered roles and expectations, these biases create barriers to entry and advancement for women in creative fields. Discrimination and prejudice based on gender identity, race, ethnicity, and other intersecting factors further exacerbate the challenges faced by women, limiting their access to opportunities and recognition.

123 | SMART LADIES OF THE 21ST CENTURY

Unequal representation and leadership

Women are often underrepresented in leadership positions and decision-making roles within the creative industries, perpetuating power imbalances and limiting their influence and visibility. Despite their talent and qualifications, women encounter glass ceilings and systemic barriers that hinder their ascent to leadership positions in areas such as film directing, music production, and publishing. The lack of diverse voices in positions of power not only stifles creativity and innovation but also perpetuates narrow and homogeneous narratives in cultural production.

Limited Access to Resources and Opportunities

Women in creative industries often face barriers to accessing essential resources and opportunities, such as funding, mentorship, and professional networks. Structural inequalities and systemic biases result in women receiving disproportionately fewer grants, funding, and investments for their creative projects compared to their male counterparts. Limited access to mentorship and networking opportunities further impedes women's career advancement, hindering their ability to access support, guidance, and opportunities for growth and collaboration.

Opportunities for Empowerment and Collective Action

Despite the challenges they face, women in the creative industries have increasingly embraced opportunities for empowerment, advocacy, and collective action to effect systemic change. Initiatives such as #MeToo and Time's Up have sparked conversations and campaigns to combat sexual harassment, gender discrimination, and inequality in the entertainment industry and beyond. Women-led organizations, networks, and alliances provide platforms for advocacy, mentorship, and support, amplifying women's voices and advocating for policy reforms to promote gender equity and inclusion in creative spaces.

Fostering Inclusive and Equitable Creative Spaces

Addressing the challenges faced by women in creative industries requires concerted efforts to dismantle systemic inequalities and create more inclusive and equitable spaces for all. By challenging gender bias and stereotypes, promoting diverse representation and leadership, and ensuring equal access to resources and opportunities, we can empower women to thrive and succeed in creative fields. Through advocacy, mentorship, and collective action, we can build a more inclusive and equitable creative ecosystem that celebrates and amplifies the talents and contributions of all creators, regardless of gender or identity.

Role of Women in Promoting Diversity and Inclusion in Cultural Settings.

Women have emerged as powerful advocates for diversity, equity, and inclusion in cultural spaces, spearheading initiatives and movements to champion representation and amplify marginalized voices. This section explores the pivotal role of women-led efforts in advancing diversity and inclusion in the arts, entertainment, and media industries. It highlights the significance of intersectional advocacy, allyship, and solidarity in fostering cultural environments that authentically reflect the richness and diversity of human experiences.

Women-Led Initiatives and Organizations

Women-led initiatives and organizations have been at the forefront of promoting diversity and inclusion in cultural spaces, advocating for equitable representation and opportunities for underrepresented communities. From grassroots movements to established advocacy groups, these initiatives work tirelessly to challenge systemic inequalities and amplify marginalized voices. Organizations such as Women in Film, Women Make Movies, and the Geena Davis Institute on Gender in Media are dedicated to advancing gender equity and representation in the entertainment industry, while initiatives like #DisabilityTooWhite and #OscarsSoWhite advocate for greater diversity and inclusion across cultural sectors.

Intersectional advocacy and representation

Intersectional advocacy recognizes the interconnectedness of social identities and experiences, advocating for the inclusion and empowerment of marginalized individuals across intersecting axes of oppression. Women leaders in cultural spaces have embraced intersectional approaches to advocacy, recognizing the importance of representing diverse perspectives and lived experiences in artistic expression and storytelling. By centering the voices and experiences of women of color, LGBTQ+ individuals, people with disabilities, and other marginalized groups, these leaders strive to create more inclusive and authentic cultural narratives that resonate with diverse audiences.

Allyship and Solidarity

Women in cultural spaces have also embraced allyship and solidarity as essential strategies for advancing diversity and inclusion. Allies actively support and amplify the voices of marginalized individuals, using their privilege and platforms to advocate for systemic change and challenge oppressive structures. Through collaborative efforts and coalitions, women allies work together to dismantle barriers, disrupt biases, and create spaces that affirm and celebrate the diversity of human experiences. By standing in solidarity with marginalized communities, women leaders pave the way for a more inclusive and equitable cultural landscape for all.

Creating Inclusive and Equitable Cultural Environments

The role of women in promoting diversity and inclusion in cultural spaces is indispensable, as they lead efforts to challenge stereotypes, amplify underrepresented voices, and foster environments that reflect the richness and complexity of human experiences. Through their leadership, advocacy, and allyship, women are driving transformative change in the arts, entertainment, and media industries, shaping cultural narratives that resonate with diverse audiences and inspire social progress. As we celebrate their contributions and commitment to diversity and inclusion, let us continue to support and uplift women-led initiatives and movements that strive to create a more inclusive and equitable cultural landscape for generations to come.

Celebrating Women's Creativity and Cultural Contributions

The contributions of women in the arts, entertainment, and media industries are as diverse and multifaceted as the women themselves. From challenging stereotypes to promoting social change, women have left an indelible mark on cultural landscapes, shaping perceptions and inspiring generations with their creativity, resilience, and vision. As we celebrate their achievements and honor their legacies, let us continue to champion the rights and representation of women in creative industries, ensuring that their voices are heard and their talents are recognized and celebrated in shaping the cultural narratives of our time.

Chapter 6

Navigating Work-Life Balance

Achieving a harmonious balance between career, family, and personal life is a perennial challenge for women in today's fast-paced world. In this chapter, we delve into the multifaceted complexities of navigating work-life balance, exploring the unique challenges faced by women, the strategies employed to achieve equilibrium, and the pivotal role of supportive workplaces and policies. Through illuminating success stories and practical resources, we aim to empower women to prioritize self-care, manage their responsibilities effectively, and cultivate fulfillment in both their professional and personal spheres.

Challenges Faced by Women in Balancing a Career, Family, and Personal Life

Balancing the demands of career, family, and personal life is a delicate tightrope walk that many women navigate daily. At the heart of this struggle lies a multitude of challenges, both systemic and personal, that often converge to create a formidable barrier to achieving work-life balance.

1. Societal Expectations and Cultural Norms:

Women often face immense pressure from societal expectations and cultural norms regarding their roles and responsibilities. Traditional gender roles dictate that women are primarily responsible for caregiving and household duties, even as they pursue careers and professional aspirations. These ingrained societal expectations can lead to feelings of guilt and inadequacy when attempting to balance career ambitions with family commitments.

2. Workplace Policies and Structures:

The rigidity of workplace policies and structures can pose significant challenges for women seeking work-life balance. Limited access to flexible work arrangements, inadequate parental leave policies, and a lack of support for caregiving responsibilities can exacerbate the juggling act faced by working women. Additionally, the prevalence of workplace cultures that prioritize long hours and constant availability can make it difficult for women to prioritize personal well-being without fear of professional repercussions.

3. Personal circumstances and responsibilities:

Individual circumstances, such as single parenthood, eldercare responsibilities, and health concerns, further complicate the quest for work-life balance. Women often find themselves grappling with the competing demands of caring for loved ones while also striving to advance their careers and pursue personal interests. The weight of these responsibilities can take a toll on mental and emotional well-being, leading to burnout and exhaustion.

4. Stigma Surrounding Caregiving Responsibilities:

Despite strides towards gender equality, caregiving responsibilities are still predominantly viewed as a woman's domain, leading to a stigma surrounding women who prioritize family over career. Women may face judgment or discrimination in the workplace for taking time off to care for children or elderly relatives, further complicating their efforts to achieve work-life balance without sacrificing professional opportunities.

5. Pervasive Guilt and Self-Imposed Pressure:

Perhaps one of the most significant challenges faced by women in balancing career, family, and personal life is the pervasive guilt and self-imposed pressure to excel in all domains simultaneously. Women often internalize societal expectations and strive for perfection, fearing that any perceived shortcomings in one area will reflect negatively on their abilities and worth. This relentless pursuit of perfection can lead to chronic stress, anxiety, and feelings of inadequacy.

The challenges faced by women in balancing career, family, and personal life are multifaceted and deeply ingrained in societal structures and norms. Addressing these challenges requires a concerted effort to dismantle systemic inequalities, advocate for supportive workplace policies, and foster a culture of empathy and understanding that values the diverse roles and responsibilities of women in modern society.

Strategies for Achieving Work-Life Balance and Prioritizing Self-care

Despite the formidable challenges posed by the quest for work-life balance, women have devised an array of strategies to navigate these complexities effectively while prioritizing their well-being. This section delves into practical strategies and techniques honed by women to maintain equilibrium amidst the demands of career, family, and personal life. From adept time management to establishing clear boundaries and embracing mindfulness practices, these strategies empower women to cultivate balance and resilience in the face of competing priorities. Moreover, the section underscores the vital importance of self-compassion, delegation, and seeking support networks to bolster well-being and foster sustainable success.

1. Time Management:

Effective time management is paramount for women seeking to achieve a work-life balance. By prioritizing tasks, setting realistic goals, and allocating time strategically, women can optimize productivity and minimize stress. Utilizing tools such as calendars, to-do lists, and time-tracking apps can aid in maintaining organization and accountability, allowing women to navigate their myriad responsibilities with greater efficiency and effectiveness.

2. Boundary Setting:

Establishing clear boundaries between work and personal life is essential for preserving mental and emotional well-being. Women can delineate specific times for work-related tasks and leisure activities, ensuring dedicated periods for relaxation. Implementing rituals such as "unplugging" from technology during non-work hours and creating designated spaces for work and leisure can reinforce boundaries and promote work-life balance.

3. Mindfulness Practices:

Mindfulness practices, such as meditation, deep breathing exercises, and mindfulness-based stress reduction techniques, offer invaluable tools for managing stress and enhancing resilience. By cultivating present-moment awareness and cultivating a non-judgmental attitude toward their experiences, women can reduce anxiety and foster greater emotional balance amidst the demands of daily life.

4. Self-Compassion:

Practicing self-compassion is essential for nurturing well-being and resilience in the face of adversity. Women can cultivate self-compassion by treating themselves with kindness and understanding, acknowledging their limitations, and reframing self-critical thoughts with compassion and empathy. Embracing self-care practices, such as engaging in hobbies, spending time with loved ones, and prioritizing rest, is vital for replenishing energy and maintaining psychological health.

5. Delegation:

Delegating tasks and responsibilities to trusted individuals or outsourcing services can alleviate the burden of excessive workload and enable women to focus on priorities that align with their values and goals. Whether delegating household chores, childcare responsibilities, or work-related tasks, women can leverage delegation as a strategic tool for optimizing efficiency and reclaiming time for self-care and personal pursuits.

6. Seeking Support Networks:

Building and nurturing support networks of friends, family members, mentors, and colleagues is crucial for navigating the challenges of work-life balance. Women can lean on their support networks for emotional support, practical assistance, and guidance in times of need. Participating in support groups, networking events, and online communities can provide valuable connections and resources for sharing experiences and seeking advice.

In essence, the pursuit of work-life balance necessitates a multifaceted approach encompassing effective time management, boundary setting, mindfulness practices, self-compassion, delegation, and seeking support networks. By embracing these strategies and prioritizing self-care, women can cultivate resilience, enhance well-being, and thrive amidst the demands of modern life.

The Significance of Policies and Workplaces that Empower Women

Supportive workplaces and policies are instrumental in enabling women to achieve work-life balance and navigate the competing demands of career and caregiving responsibilities. This section elucidates the profound impact of organizational culture, flexible work arrangements, parental leave policies, and childcare support on women's ability to balance their professional and personal lives effectively. It underscores the transformative benefits of inclusive workplace practices that prioritize diversity, equity, and work-life integration, fostering environments characterized by trust, respect, and employee well-being.

1. Organizational Culture:

The culture of an organization profoundly influences its employees' experiences and perceptions of work-life balance. Cultivating a supportive organizational culture that values work-life balance fosters employee satisfaction, engagement, and retention. Organizations that prioritize employee well-being through initiatives such as flexible work arrangements, wellness programs, and recognition of caregiving responsibilities cultivate a culture of trust and respect, empowering women to thrive in their professional roles while maintaining fulfilling personal lives.

2. Flexible Work Arrangements:

Flexible work arrangements, such as telecommuting, flextime, and compressed workweeks, afford employees greater autonomy and control over their work schedules, facilitating work-life balance. By accommodating diverse needs and lifestyles, flexible work arrangements enable women to tailor their work hours to accommodate caregiving responsibilities, personal commitments, and lifestyle preferences. Moreover, flexible work arrangements enhance productivity, job satisfaction, and employee morale, contributing to organizational success and competitiveness in the global marketplace.

3. Parental Leave Policies:

Comprehensive parental leave policies are essential for supporting working parents, including women, during significant life transitions such as childbirth and adoption. Paid parental leave policies provide employees with the necessary time and financial support to bond with their newborns, adjust to parenthood, and return to work with confidence. By offering equitable and inclusive parental leave benefits, organizations demonstrate their commitment to supporting employees' work-life balance and fostering a family-friendly workplace culture.

4. Childcare Support:

Access to affordable, high-quality childcare is paramount for working parents, particularly women, who often shoulder the bulk of caregiving responsibilities. Employers can support working parents by offering on-site childcare facilities, subsidies for childcare expenses, and referral services to reputable childcare providers. By alleviating the logistical and financial burdens associated with childcare, organizations empower women to pursue their professional aspirations while ensuring the well-being and development of their children.

5. Work-Life Integration:

Embracing a philosophy of work-life integration, as opposed to strict delineations between work and personal life, promotes holistic well-being and fulfillment among employees. Organizations that recognize and accommodate employees' multifaceted identities and priorities foster a culture of work-life integration, wherein employees are encouraged to bring their whole selves to work and pursue meaningful personal and professional endeavors. By promoting work-life integration, organizations support women in achieving balance, satisfaction, and success in all aspects of their lives.

In conclusion, supportive workplaces and policies are essential enablers of work-life balance for women, providing the foundation for success, fulfillment, and well-being. By prioritizing organizational culture, flexible work arrangements, parental leave policies, childcare support, and work-life integration, organizations can create inclusive, equitable, and empowering environments where women can thrive personally and professionally.

Success Stories of Women Who Have Found Work-life Balance and Fulfilment

Within the labyrinth of work-life balance, there exist countless narratives of women who have forged paths illuminated by harmony, fulfillment, and success. This section serves as a testament to the resilience, ingenuity, and tenacity of women who have navigated the intricate terrain of balancing career, family, and personal aspirations with grace and determination.

Through the profiles of these remarkable individuals, we glean insights into their strategies, experiences, and triumphs, offering inspiration and guidance to those embarking on similar journeys.

1. Dr. Maya Patel: Juggling a Demanding Career and Family, Dr. Maya Patel, a renowned neurosurgeon, and mother of two, epitomizes the epitome of balancing a demanding career with family responsibilities. Despite the rigors of her profession, Dr. Patel has prioritized her family's well-being, maintaining open communication with her spouse and children, and carving out quality time for cherished moments together. Through meticulous planning, effective time management, and unwavering dedication, Dr. Patel has successfully harmonized her professional achievements with her role as a loving wife and mother, embodying the essence of work-life balance.

2. Sarah Thompson: From Corporate Executive to Entrepreneurial Freedom, Sarah Thompson's journey from a high-powered corporate executive to

a successful entrepreneur reflects the transformative power of pursuing one's passions and priorities. After years of climbing the corporate ladder, Sarah felt unfulfilled and burned out, yearning for greater autonomy and purpose in her life. Leveraging her expertise and entrepreneurial spirit, Sarah embarked on a new chapter, founding her sustainable fashion brand that aligned with her values and aspirations. By prioritizing her well-being, creativity, and authenticity, Sarah has discovered a newfound sense of fulfillment and balance, demonstrating the liberating potential of following one's heart and dreams.

3. Maria Rodriguez: Navigating the Dual Role of Carer and Career Woman, Maria Rodriguez's journey as a devoted carer and career woman underscores the inherent challenges and rewards of balancing multiple roles and responsibilities. As the primary carer for her aging parents, while simultaneously pursuing a demanding career in

finance, Maria has confronted myriad challenges with resilience and grace. Through strategic delegation, boundary-setting, and unwavering determination, Maria has successfully managed her dual roles, finding fulfillment and purpose in both her professional and personal endeavors. Her unwavering commitment to her family and career exemplifies the profound impact of perseverance and prioritizing what matters most in life.

4. Dr. Li Wei: Cultivating Work-Life Integration as an Academic Leader, Dr. Li Wei, a distinguished academic leader and mother of three, embodies the principles of work-life integration, fostering a harmonious balance between her professional and personal pursuits. As a trailblazing researcher and mentor in the field of environmental science, Dr. Wei has championed innovative approaches to fostering work-life balance within her academic institution. Through flexible work arrangements, supportive policies, and a culture of

mutual respect and understanding, Dr. Wei has empowered her colleagues to thrive personally and professionally while achieving groundbreaking research outcomes. Her visionary leadership and commitment to holistic well-being serve as a beacon of inspiration for women in academia and beyond.

These stories represent a tapestry of resilience, determination, and fulfillment, showcasing the myriad ways in which women can navigate the complexities of work-life balance with grace and purpose. Through their experiences and insights, these women illuminate the path forward, offering invaluable lessons and inspiration for all those seeking harmony and fulfillment in their lives.

Resources and Tips for Managing Work-Life Integration

Empowering women with practical resources and actionable strategies is essential for navigating the intricate landscape of work-life integration successfully. This section serves as a comprehensive guide, offering a curated selection of resources and insightful tips designed to equip women with the tools and support needed to harmonize their professional and personal spheres effectively.

1. Books:

"The Four Agreements" by Don Miguel Ruiz:

This transformative book offers timeless wisdom and practical insights for cultivating balance, happiness, and fulfillment in all areas of life.

"The Power of Now" by Eckhart Tolle:

Through mindfulness and presence, Tolle's teachings empower individuals to transcend past regrets and future anxieties, fostering a deeper sense of peace and inner harmony.

"Daring Greatly" by Brené Brown:

Brown's groundbreaking work explores the power of vulnerability and courage, inspiring women to embrace authenticity, connection, and wholehearted living.

2. **Podcasts:**

"The Work-Life Balance Podcast," hosted by Rick Monaro:

This podcast provides actionable tips and inspiring stories from experts and thought leaders on achieving work-life balance and prioritizing well-being.

"The Balanced Life" with Robin Long:

Focused on holistic health and wellness, this podcast offers practical advice and mindful practices for women seeking to integrate work, fitness, and self-care into their daily lives.

3. Online Courses:

"Work-Life Balance Mastery" by Udemy:

This comprehensive online course offers practical strategies and tools for achieving work-life balance, managing stress, and prioritizing self-care.

"Mindfulness-Based Stress Reduction (MBSR)" by Coursera:

Developed by mindfulness pioneer Jon Kabat-Zinn, this course teaches mindfulness techniques to reduce stress, enhance resilience, and cultivate well-being in daily life.

4. Support Networks:

Lean in Circles:

Lean in Circles provides a supportive community for women to connect, share experiences, and empower each other to pursue their professional and personal goals with confidence and resilience.

Women's Leadership Networks:

To promote professional development, networking, and mentoring opportunities for women at all career stages, numerous organizations offer affinity groups and women's leadership networks.

5. Practical Tips and Strategies:

Prioritize self-care:

Schedule regular self-care activities, such as exercise, meditation, or hobbies, to recharge and replenish your energy reserves.

Set boundaries:

Establish clear boundaries between work and personal life and communicate them effectively to colleagues and family members to protect your time and well-being.

Delegate tasks:

Delegate tasks and responsibilities where possible, both at work and at home, to alleviate overwhelm and create space for activities that bring you joy and fulfillment.

Practice mindfulness:

Incorporate mindfulness practices into your daily routine, such as mindful breathing, body scans, or gratitude journaling, to cultivate present-moment awareness and reduce stress.

Through utilizing these resources and putting useful advice and techniques into practice, women may equip themselves to deal with the challenges of balancing work and life with resilience, self-assurance, and overall well-being.

Every woman can navigate work-life balance by starting the trip with intention, resilience, and self-compassion. The path will have ups and downs, victories and losses. Women can enhance their sense of balance, fulfillment, and well-being beyond the confines of work and personal life by recognizing the obstacles, adopting practical solutions, supporting encouraging work environments, and taking inspiration from the achievements of others. Let's prioritize self-care, build resilience, and create conditions that enable women to thrive in all facets of their lives as we continue to manage the challenges of modern living.

Chapter 7

Empowering Future Generations

Empowering the next generation of women is a necessary step toward building a more successful and equitable society. The efforts and initiatives forming the next generation of female leaders are examined as this chapter explores the value of education, mentoring, and community support for young women. This chapter makes a strong case for supporting and mentoring the girls and young women who will lead us into the future by highlighting mentors and role models and outlining methods for achieving gender equality.

Comprehending the significance of these endeavors demands a review of the obstacles encountered by women in advocacy and politics, **which are discussed in Chapter Four**. Systemic obstacles, such as discrimination, underrepresentation, and gender prejudice, have long plagued women in politics. These difficulties are not unique; rather, they are part of a larger framework that has an impact on women in several fields, such as mentoring and education.

The political sphere, which presents a unique set of challenges, is a reflection of the larger social difficulties that women encounter. For the upcoming generation, female political leaders and activists who have dedicated their lives to dismantling barriers and granting a platform to women's voices may impart invaluable knowledge on perseverance and tactical methods of surmounting challenges. Educational and mentorship programs targeted towards young women can be informed and inspired by their strategic tactics, such as coalition-building and resilience in the face of gender prejudice in politics.

Women find it difficult to get together and fight for shared objectives because of historical issues like artificial borders and divide-and-rule strategies imposed by colonial powers. The form of political institutions and the possibilities open to women have been shaped by these historical legacies. For programs that enable young women to negotiate and confront the political environment to be designed effectively, it is imperative to understand these dynamics.

In addition, young women are inspired and guided into leadership positions by the tremendous role models that are the accomplishments of women in politics and advocacy. These leaders are models of the bravery, tenacity, and strategic thought required to bring about change. We can provide young women with the resources they need to excel in a variety of industries by incorporating the lessons learned from these trailblazers into mentoring and educational initiatives.

Being educated is a vital first step toward empowerment. To close the gender gap, programs aimed at giving females access to high-quality education—especially in STEM fields—are crucial. To promote gender equality, programs that inspire girls to seek higher education and professions in sectors that have historically been dominated by men are essential.

Education and mentoring have complementary roles. For young women, having mentors who can offer direction, encouragement, and practical counsel is priceless. Mentors provide insights rarely found in textbooks, assisting young women in navigating the difficulties of their chosen industries.

Furthermore, young women's goals and confidence are greatly influenced by the support of their communities, which lays the groundwork for their development and success. Encouraging and supporting peer, family, and community contexts for young women may have a big influence on their goals and self-esteem. Social and economic hurdles can be surmounted by young women through community-based programs that unite them and provide them access to networks and resources.

We also identify certain efforts and programs in this chapter that have effectively empowered young women. These include grassroots organizations, advocacy groups, leadership development programs, and scholarships. You may identify best practices and scalable, reproducible solutions through the analysis of these successful models, which will eventually have a larger effect.

The tenacity, bravery, and unyielding spirit of young women who fearlessly dream large and demolish barriers are ultimately honored in this chapter. It is a testament to their potential as well as a call to action for the next generation to continue the fight for female autonomy and gender equity in all spheres of life. Together, we can deconstruct barriers and build a future where women can lead and succeed without boundaries by offering the education, mentorship, and community support that are required.

Exploring political activism and educational empowerment enables a comprehensive understanding of strategies for fostering independence and equity and the interconnectedness of education, mentorship, and community support.

Importance of Mentorship, Education, and Community Support

In the quest to empower young women, mentorship, education, and community support serve as foundations that provide them with the know-how and direction, they need to reach their full potential. This section explores how mentorship programs, inclusive educational efforts, and supportive communities may foster the aspirations and skills of girls and young women globally in a meaningful and revolutionary way. Through the provision of role models, educational opportunities, and support networks, these interventions act as catalysts for women's future success and leadership.

Transformative Impact of Mentorship Programs

Young women's paths are significantly shaped by mentoring programs, which provide them with priceless direction, support, and insight as they negotiate the challenges of both personal and professional development. These programs give young women the chance to benefit from the experiences and knowledge of seasoned professionals by matching mentees with mentors who have a wealth of experience and who can offer guidance, support, and insights. As mentees pursue their objectives and dreams, mentorship instills confidence and resilience in them by fostering a sense of belonging, empowerment, and aspiration—whether in academic, professional, or community settings.

Inclusive Education Initiatives

To ensure that all young women have equal access to high-quality learning opportunities and possibilities for both intellectual and personal growth, inclusive education efforts are crucial. These programs aim to address systemic prejudices and hurdles that may impede girls' and young women's academic and socio-emotional development by fostering diversity, equity, and inclusion in educational environments. Inclusive education projects aim to establish spaces where every young woman feels respected, encouraged, and empowered to follow her interests and passions without boundaries, whether through curriculum modifications, mentorship programs, or scholarships.

Supportive Communities: Nurturing Growth and Resilience

Young women need supportive groups to help them grow and develop because they give them a sense of community, companionship, and support when they face chances and challenges in life. These communities, which can be found in homes, schools, or peer groups, provide young women with a secure and supportive environment in which they can express who they are, explore their interests, and build deep connections with people who share their goals and beliefs. Supportive communities help young women develop resilience, self-confidence, and a sense of agency by fostering collective empowerment and solidarity. This gives them the resources and encouragement they need to face challenges head-on and courageously follow their aspirations.

Community support, education, and mentoring are essential pillars in the process of empowering young women and helping them realize their full potential. Investing in inclusive education initiatives, supportive communities, and mentorship programs may establish conditions that enable every girl and young woman to flourish, succeed, and lead with resilience and confidence. Together, we can create a future in which gender equality is not only an ideal but also a reality, allowing every young woman to follow her dreams and passions without limitations.

Project and Activities Empowering Young Girls and Women

Programs and initiatives aimed at empowering young women and girls have become essential tools for advancing their potential as leaders and for personal and professional development. The efforts and best practices that are geared towards providing girls and young women with the tools, knowledge, and chances necessary to succeed in a variety of fields are highlighted in this area.

These initiatives, which range from STEM education programs to leadership development programs, are crucial in clearing the path for a future that is more inclusive and egalitarian.

STEM Education Programs: Opening Doors to Opportunities

Programs that teach girls and young women about STEM (science, technology, engineering, and mathematics) are essential for removing barriers and increasing their chances in historically male-dominated areas. Through practical learning opportunities, exposure to female role models, and connections to supportive networks, these programs seek to develop girls' interest, confidence, and skill in STEM disciplines from an early age. These projects help close the gender gap in STEM professions and unleash the unrealized potential of young women in driving technological innovation and advancement by enabling girls to see themselves as future scientists, engineers, and inventors and by encouraging a love for STEM disciplines.

Leadership Development Initiatives: Cultivating Future Leaders

By giving girls and young women the abilities, information, and self-assurance necessary to succeed as leaders in their communities and beyond, leadership development programs play a critical role in fostering their potential as leaders. Girls are given the tools to find their voice, push for change, and have a positive social impact through these programs that provide networking, mentoring, and leadership training. These programs prepare a new generation of female leaders capable of taking on difficult tasks and bringing about significant change in a variety of social contexts by promoting traits like resilience, empathy, and inclusion.

Entrepreneurship and Economic Empowerment Programs

Girls and young women are given the tools and resources necessary to unleash their entrepreneurial spirit and attain financial independence through entrepreneurship and economic empowerment programs. These programs provide access to money, networking opportunities, mentorship, and training in entrepreneurship, financial literacy, and business skills. Through the promotion of an entrepreneurial attitude and the provision of business venture support, these projects help young women and girls surmount obstacles to economic involvement and pave the road for their own and their communities' success.

Advocacy and Empowerment Campaigns: Amplifying Voices

Campaigns for empowerment and advocacy are effective means of elevating the voices and perspectives of young women and girls, bringing attention to issues affecting their rights and welfare, and igniting a movement for change. These initiatives aim to challenge societal norms and stereotypes that support gender inequality, advocate for policy reforms, and address issues including gender-based violence, access to education, and reproductive health rights. These projects enable girls and young women to become change agents and advocates for gender equality in their communities and beyond by giving them a platform for advocacy and activism.

In conclusion, efforts and programs aimed at empowering young women and girls are crucial for advancing social inclusion and gender equality. Through the provision of educational, leadership, entrepreneurial, and advocacy opportunities, these initiatives empower girls and young women to reach their full potential, make significant contributions to society, and mold a fairer and more inclusive future for everybody.

Mentors and Role Models Inspiring the Next Generation

Mentors and role models act as beacons of light, providing the next generation of female leaders with direction, support, and inspiration. Girls and young women who aspire to make a difference in the world can find inspiration and advice from these remarkable women, who have established themselves as leaders and changemakers in their respective industries. These role models—from visionary activists to trailblazing entrepreneurs— exemplify courage, resiliency, and enthusiasm, motivating people to follow their passions and make a good impact in their communities and beyond.

Trailblazing Entrepreneurs: Pioneering Paths to Success

Pioneering businesspeople create successful routes in the face of difficulties and hardship, acting as living examples of inventiveness, resiliency, and willpower. With their audacious ideas and spirit of entrepreneurship, these women have disrupted entire sectors, broken through glass ceilings, and defied expectations as company founders. By sharing their experiences of success and failure, they enable prospective business owners to take calculated risks, grab hold of life's possibilities, and never give up on their goals. This allows them to successfully negotiate the challenges of entrepreneurship and reach their full potential as innovators and leaders.

Visionary Activists: Advocating for Change

Visionary activists lead movements for change and challenge the status quo to create a more just and equitable world. They are unwavering advocates for social justice, equity, and human rights. These women are leading initiatives to combat systemic injustices, strengthen marginalized communities, and advance the rights and dignity of all people, serving as both grassroots organizers and international champions. They encourage others to take up the cause of justice and equality by fearlessly confronting authority and fostering group action, kindling a passion for activism and advocacy among young women worldwide.

Inspirational Leaders: Making a Difference

Leaders who inspire others originate from diverse backgrounds and uphold principles of honesty, kindness, and understanding in their positions of authority. These women lead with vision, purpose, and a dedication to helping others, whether they are in business, politics, academia, or community service. They empower girls and young women to embrace their unique strengths, follow their passions, and lead with courage and conviction. By setting an example and showcasing the power of authentic and inclusive leadership, they equip them to become tomorrow's leaders and effect positive change in their communities and beyond.

Mentors and role models are essential in motivating and directing the upcoming generation of female leaders by providing priceless advice, inspiration, and support during the process. These inspiring women encourage girls and young women to believe in themselves, follow their passions, and embrace their potential to change the world by sharing their experiences, knowledge, and skills. They clear the path for a day when all girls and young women can strive to fulfill their aspirations and make significant contributions to society through their mentoring and leadership.

Strategies for Promoting Gender Equality and Empowering Girls

Advocating for gender parity and empowering young women requires many approaches focused on tearing down prejudices and obstacles that prevent them from pursuing chances, higher education, and leadership positions. This section explores many strategies and projects that people and groups can implement to promote a more just and inclusive society in which every girl has the chance to reach her full potential.

Advocating for Policy Changes: Ensuring Equal Opportunities

One of the most important steps in advancing gender equality and fostering an atmosphere that supports girls' empowerment is advocating for legislative changes. This entails advocating for legislative changes that target institutional impediments and biased behaviors in sectors like social welfare, employment, healthcare, and education. To level the playing field and allow girls to follow their dreams freely, policies that support equal access to education, prevent gender-based violence, and protect reproductive rights are crucial.

Challenging Stereotypes and Cultural Norms: Redefining Gender Roles

Changing societal attitudes and behaviors towards more inclusivity and acceptance of girls' skills and aspirations requires challenging stereotypes and cultural norms that support gender inequity. This means spreading good images of girls and women in the media and popular culture, questioning conventional ideas of femininity and masculinity, and encouraging empathy and critical thinking in people of all genders. To foster a more encouraging and welcoming atmosphere where females feel free to follow their interests and goals without being constrained by their gender, society should work to dispel misconceptions and promote gender-positive messaging.

Fostering Supportive Environments: Creating Safe Spaces

It is imperative to establish surroundings that are supportive and foster girls' agency, self-worth, and confidence to enable them to flourish. This entails creating peer support groups, mentorship programs, and safe spaces where girls may express themselves, exchange stories, and get help and direction. Girls can receive the support and motivation they require to follow their dreams, grow as leaders, and stand up for their rights and interests from schools, community centers, and youth organizations.

Investing in Education and Skills Development: Unlocking Potential

It is critical to invest in girls' education and skill development to fully realize their potential and position them for leadership and financial independence. This entails making certain that all girls have equitable access to high-quality schooling, career training, and STEM programs that provide them with the information, abilities, and self-assurance to follow a variety of career routes and make significant contributions to society. Moreover, initiatives to advance financial literacy, entrepreneurial education, and digital literacy can provide women with the knowledge and assets they need to meet the demands of the modern economy and achieve their goals.

In conclusion, promoting gender equality and empowering girls require concerted efforts across multiple fronts, including advocacy for policy changes, challenging stereotypes, fostering supportive environments, and investing in education and skills development. By addressing systemic barriers and biases and creating opportunities for girls to thrive, society can harness the full potential of girls and young women as agents of change and leaders in building a more just, equitable, and inclusive world.

Opportunities for Individuals and Organizations to Support Future Generations

Future generations of women can be greatly aided and inspired by individuals and organizations, creating an atmosphere in which girls can flourish and realize their full potential. The following section highlights concrete actions and avenues for individuals and organizations to support the progress and empowerment of girls and young women:

Individual Opportunities for Support and Mentorship:

Everyone has the power to positively impact girls' lives by providing them with support, direction, and mentoring. This can be helping out at youth organizations, acting as mentors or role models, and giving ladies who are pursuing their aspirations advice and encouragement. People may support females to overcome barriers, follow their passions, and achieve their goals by sharing their experiences, knowledge, and skills.

Advocacy and Awareness-Raising Efforts:

To promote systemic change and increase public understanding of the significance of gender equality and girls' empowerment, advocacy and awareness-raising initiatives are crucial. People can utilize their networks and platforms to support campaigns and projects that advance girls' rights and opportunities, support policy reforms, and elevate the voices of young women and girls. One way that people can help create a more fair and inclusive society for future generations is by supporting gender-inclusive legislation and speaking out against discriminatory practices and attitudes.

Financial Support and Investment:

For girls and young women to have greater access to education, skill development, and economic possibilities, financial support and investment are essential. Through scholarships, grants, and gifts to institutions that serve underprivileged populations and offer educational resources, individuals can promote the education of girls. A more just and prosperous future for all can be fostered by individuals funding initiatives and programs that support girls' economic empowerment, leadership development, and entrepreneurial endeavors.

Corporate and Philanthropic Initiatives:

The advancement of gender equality and the creation of opportunities for girls and young women are greatly aided by corporate and charitable endeavors. In addition to investing in girls' education and skill-training programs, businesses can adopt policies and practices that encourage women's leadership and career advancement. They can also support community-based projects that cater to the particular demands and difficulties that young women and girls experience. Likewise, charitable institutions can provide funding for initiatives and plans that empower women, advance gender parity, and remove structural obstacles to girls' empowerment and education.

It is the collective duty of individuals and institutions to encourage and elevate upcoming generations of women to establish a society where every girl can flourish and reach her full potential. Through the strategic utilization of their assets, connections, and clout, people and organizations can help create a future that is more just, inclusive, and prosperous for everybody.

It is not just a question of social justice but also of achieving our societies' and economies' full potential, we must empower the next generation of women. We can build a more promising and just future for all by supporting female leadership, gender equality, and education while also investing in mentorship, education, and community assistance. This chapter is meant to act as a call to action for the girls and young women who will be the future leaders of our society.

Conclusion

To sum up, the chapters in this book provide a thorough summary of how women's achievement and empowerment have changed in the twenty-first century. Women have shown their tenacity, inventiveness, and unrelenting resolve to create a more just and inclusive world by shattering glass ceilings in corporate boardrooms and producing ground-breaking discoveries in scientific labs.

The book explores the complex lives of women in a variety of fields, such as business, science, politics, the arts, and advocacy, showcasing their accomplishments, struggles, and achievements. It emphasizes how crucial it is to acknowledge and celebrate the variety of skills and accomplishments possessed by women, as well as the institutional prejudices and roadblocks that still stand in the way of their advancement.

The chapters' recurring themes of education, community support, mentoring, and group action highlight how important these elements are to enabling women and girls to realize their full potential. Individuals and organizations can help create a more just, equitable, and successful society for all by encouraging inclusive environments, advocating for gender equality, and funding girls' education and empowerment.

In the end, the stories told in this book are a monument to the unwavering energy and tenacity of women, who persistently shatter preconceptions, challenge expectations, and open doors for upcoming generations. Let us be motivated by their experiences and resolve to build a world in which every woman and girl has the chance to prosper and leave her mark on the world as we look to the future.

References and Resources

Books:

1. "Lean In: Women, Work, and the Will to Lead" by Sheryl Sandberg

2. "Inferior: How Science Got Women Wrong—and the New Research That's Rewriting the Story" by Angela Saini

3. "The Confidence Code: The Science and Art of Self-Assurance— What Women Should Know" by Katty Kay and Claire Shipman

4. "Women and Power: A Manifesto" by Mary Beard

5. "The Moment of Lift: How Empowering Women Changes the World" by Melinda Gates

Articles and Research Papers:

1. "Closing the Gender Gap: Act Now"— World Economic Forum Report

2. "The State of Women in Tech 2021" (AnitaB.org Report)

3. "Gender Equality and Women's Empowerment: A Critical Analysis of the Third Millennium Development Goal" (United Nations Development Program)

4. "The Impact of COVID-19 on Women: Spotlight on Employment" (International Labor Organization)

5. "Gender Differences in Science, Technology, Engineering, and Mathematics (STEM) Interest, Credits Earned, and NAEP

Concerning women's empowerment, gender equality, and diversity in a range of fields, these sites provide an extensive array of materials for more research and discovery. These references offer insightful information to assist ongoing learning and advocacy activities, whether they are books, articles, research papers, or organizations committed to expanding women's rights and opportunities.

About the Author

My name is Eddie A. Opitz, and I have a strong passion for writing, creativity, and entrepreneurship. I've set out on a quest to investigate the complex field of women's empowerment in the twenty-first century because I sincerely want to have a positive influence on the world. Through my work, I hope to motivate others to support gender equality and inclusivity and to highlight the incredible accomplishments of women in a variety of fields.

I want to use narrative to highlight the opportunities and difficulties that women in today's society confront, drawing on my experiences and passions for writing and creating. As a socially conscious entrepreneur with an eye for innovation, I firmly believe that enabling women to reach their full potential and make significant contributions to both their local communities and society as a whole can impact lives.

With **"Smart Ladies of the 21st Century,"** I seek to harness the power of words and ideas to ignite conversations, provoke thought, and catalyze action Through **"Smart Ladies of the 21st Century,"** I hope to spark ideas, encourage reflection, and inspire action in the direction of a more inclusive and fair future. With this book, I want to encourage readers to stand with me in promoting gender parity, honoring women's accomplishments, and creating conditions that allow everyone to grow and prosper.

www.ingramcontent.com/pod-product-compliance
Lightning Source LLC
Chambersburg PA
CBHW050058230526
45470CB00004B/1580